Unsafe Space

Unsafe Space

The Crisis of Free Speech on Campus

Edited by

Tom Slater

Editor
Tom Slater
spiked
London, UK

ISBN 978-1-137-58785-5   ISBN 978-1-137-58786-2 (eBook)
DOI 10.1057/978-1-137-58786-2

Cover illustration: © Freddie Darke

Printed on acid-free paper

This Palgrave Macmillan imprint is published by Springer Nature.
The registered company is Macmillan Publishers Ltd. London.

Contents

Notes on Contributors

Sean Collins is a writer based in New York. He is US correspondent for *spiked*, writing on issues ranging from politics and race to free speech and the culture wars. Sean also blogs at americansituation.com.

Frank Furedi is a sociologist and social commentator. He has written widely on issues related to risk, health, parenting, education and free speech. His books include *The Power of Reading*, *On Tolerance*, *Authority* and *Where Have All the Intellectuals Gone?*. Frank regularly contributes to radio and television, both in the UK and internationally.

Greg Lukianoff is a constitutional lawyer and the president and CEO of the Foundation for Individual Rights in Education (FIRE), a US organisation committed to defending free speech and basic rights in higher education. He is the author of *Unlearning Liberty* and *Freedom from Speech* and has written for a range of publications including the *Atlantic*, the *Washington Post*, the *Wall Street Journal* and the *New York Times*.

Nancy McDermott is an independent researcher with a special interest in the family, parenting, science and the public and private spheres. She writes regularly on issues relating to women and the family for *spiked*. She is a non-academic affiliate of the Centre for Parenting Culture Studies at the University of Kent, and is former head and an advisor to Park Slope Parents.

Jon O'Brien is the president of Catholics for Choice, a leading US-based pro-choice organisation advocating for sexual and reproductive rights. He has worked on pro-choice advocacy on five continents to develop new ways to discuss and advance respect for women's choices. Jon has written for the *New York Times*, *The Economist*, the *International Herald Tribune* and the *Independent*, and has appeared on CNN and the BBC.

Brendan O'Neill is the editor of *spiked* and a founder of *spiked*'s transatlantic Free Speech Now! campaign. He is also a columnist for the *Big Issue*, a writer for the *Spectator*, and has contributed to the *Wall Street Journal*, the *National Review* and *USA Today*. In 2014 he was nominated for the Columnist of the Year Award at the Press Publishing Awards. He is also the author of *A Duty to Offend*, an edited collection of his essays.

Tom Slater is deputy editor at *spiked*. He coordinates *spiked*'s free-speech campaigns Down With Campus Censorship! and the Free Speech University Rankings, the UK's first university league table for free speech. Tom has written on politics, pop culture and free speech for the *Spectator*, the *Telegraph*, the *Times Higher Education*, *The Times* and the *Independent*. He also regularly appears on UK TV and radio.

Joanna Williams is an education editor at *spiked* and a regular contributor to the *Times Higher Education* and the *Guardian Higher Education Network*. She is the author of *Consuming Higher Education: Why Learning Can't Be Bought* and *Academic Freedom in an Age of Conformity: Confronting the Fear of Knowledge*.

Peter Wood is the president of the National Association of Scholars (NAS), a US network of academics and citizens that campaigns for academic freedom. He was previously a tenured member of the anthropology department at Boston University. Peter is the author of *A Bee in the Mouth: Anger in America Now* and *Diversity: The Invention of a Concept*, and has written for a range of journals and publications.

Introduction: Reinvigorating the Spirit of '64

Tom Slater

> It isn't nice to block the doorway,
> It isn't nice to go to jail,
> There are nicer ways to do it,
> But the nice ways always fail.
> It isn't nice, it isn't nice,
> You told us once, you told us twice,
> But if that is freedom's price,
> We don't mind.[1]

These lyrics, written by Malvina Reynolds, were performed by a student from atop a blockaded police car in Sproul Plaza at the University of California, Berkeley, in 1964.[2] They encapsulate the steely, optimistic atmosphere of the Free Speech Movement (FSM), Berkeley's student rebellion against the university bureaucrats who severely limited students' ability to speak freely and organise politically on campus.

Berkeley's FSMers were sick of being coddled. So much did they desire to speak out, to play their part in rethinking and reshaping their world, that they were willing to risk it all. Thankfully, it paid off. After months of suspensions, negotiations, sit-ins, arrests and strikes, they prevailed. The university's *in loco parentis* responsibilities were lifted and a generation of students across the US and Europe were inspired to agitate for their own liberation.

While the FSM produced some great orators, FSM leader Mario Savio towering above them all, Reynolds' words, in their own folksy way, epitomise the spirit of the time. In 1964, students demanded to be taken seriously as autonomous beings, capable of negotiating their academic, political and social lives away from the tutelage of their tweeded minders. Their demand for free speech was an assertion of their resilience and resolve. They didn't want to be looked after, and if getting kicked out, blacklisted or having their collars felt was what it would take to make their point, then so be it. 'If that is freedom's price, we don't mind.'

How long ago that feels. FSMers refused to be wrapped in cotton wool – today's students insist upon it. In the US and the UK, student groups routinely call for edgy speakers to be disinvited, offensive books to be banned and course syllabi to be slapped with trigger warnings. Vast swathes of speech and expression are silenced in the name of creating a 'Safe Space' where 'fragile' students can be protected from insult, upset, offence or challenge.

Over the past few years, campus censorship has reached epidemic levels. In 2015, *spiked*, the magazine I work for, launched the Free Speech University Rankings, the UK's first free-speech league table.[3] Developed by myself and a team of student researchers, the rankings found that 80 per cent of universities and students' unions have censored speech, and that the vast majority of campus bans came from student leaders. In the US, things aren't much better. The Foundation for Individual Rights in Education's (FIRE) 2015 report found that over 55 per cent of colleges substantially restricted speech.[4]

This is a tragedy. Universities should be places for thinking the unthinkable and saying the unsayable. This new intolerance poses a threat not only to students, but to the entire, truth-seeking mission of the academy. Of course, there was no golden age for free speech on campus. Before and since the FSM, free speech has faced new threats and challenges. But there is something distinct and dangerous about the contemporary crisis. In the past, campus censorship was used to silence perceived ideological threats. Today, censorship has come to be seen as a moral obligation – a necessary part of protecting thin-skinned students from the harm of words themselves. Once, universities censored ideas they were worried might catch on. Today, they censor anything that might make students 'feel uncomfortable'.

It is this shift that has made contemporary campus censorship so indiscriminate – and, quite often, unintentionally hilarious. In the past few years, universities have taken to banning pop songs, sombreros and, at one US college, 'inappropriately directed laughter'.[5] But as tempting as it is to, er, laugh it off, this is deadly serious. Free speech is the means through which we develop as autonomous beings, understand the world around us and work out how best to change it. Universities should be engines of understanding, discovery and enlightenment. But it's becoming impossible to have a casual conversation on campus, let alone a forthright debate.

spiked has been writing and campaigning on this issue for all of its 15 years. And the madness that confronts us only affirms what we free-speech fundamentalists have been saying since the beginning: that if you turn a blind eye to censorship it will only spread and spread. Now that feminists are censored in the same breath as fascists and political correctness has become entrenched, there's no more time to be complacent.

We need to remake the case for free speech on campus. We need to insist that silencing the opposition is both a cop-out and a curse. And we need to reinvigorate a belief in the ideas of truth and progress that under-pin freedom of speech. This book, bringing together writers, academics, lawyers, campaigners and activists from both the US and UK, will, we hope, be a vital contribution to that endeavour. But, more than that, we hope to dig a little deeper, trace the battle lines and unpick the myriad trends that have fed into the stifling status quo.

The recent explosion of intolerance has brought the issue of campus censorship to international attention. Campus bans make newspaper headlines, spark huge open-letter campaigns and fuel hashtag wars the world over. But even as the monomaniacal excesses of the campus thought police have generated their own kickback, the full breadth of the issue isn't always grasped. Now that even seemingly respectable figures, like Bill Maher or Germaine Greer, are being smeared and cen-sored, it's all too easy to pick our fights, dwell on the easy arguments and defend only the most socially acceptable targets.

In this book, we cover the key free-speech scandals that are so often passed over. I explore the war on lad and frat culture, and how the spurious campus rape panic is leading to the regulation of students' sex lives. Sean Collins argues that the Boycott Divestment and Sanctions (BDS) movement against Israel has chilled discussion and fuelled anti-Semitism on campus. Jon O'Brien discusses how the censorship of debate about abortion has undermined the principles of conscience and choice. Greg Lukianoff explains why trigger warnings are obliterating scholarship in the name of mental health. And Peter Wood exposes the academic policing of the so-called climate-change consensus.

Beyond probing taboos, we hope to offer some much-needed historical perspective. It's tempting to see these illiberal students as a generational blip – or a science experiment gone wrong. In truth, they are only the bastard offspring of an academic, political and social culture that has ditched and derided liberal principles – and this is something the authors here elucidate. Nancy McDermott looks at how the 1970s feminist slo-gan 'the personal is political' has fuelled campus victim culture. Joanna

Williams argues that academics have fed students the censorious ideas they are now putting into practice. And Brendan O'Neill offers a short history of liberals' complicity in campus censorship and in the diminution of moral autonomy.

There are new threats to campus freedom today. In the UK, the most immediate concern is government programmes designed to crack down on Islamist extremism through requiring universities to ban speakers and snitch on their students. But, as I argue in my chapter about counterterror measures on campus, today even state censorship is informed by a broader cultural malaise in which liberal, democratic values are not only undermined, but utterly hollowed out. While many have been outraged by the illiberal campus mob, or the state's attempt to regulate the marketplace of ideas, too few seem capable of articulating a firm, principled defence of free speech and academic freedom. This is the real problem that confronts us.

In the final chapter in this collection, Frank Furedi posits that open debate is not only necessary to make universities welcoming and stimulating environments, but is essential to the very process of intellectual and scientific progress. This is key. When we discuss campus censorship, it is our academic, intellectual and political future that is really at stake.

In the spirit of the FSM, students need to insist that understanding and changing the world means embracing resilience over victimhood, and expanding freedom rather than limiting it. We need to make every university an Unsafe Space.

Tom Slater *is deputy editor at* spiked *and coordinator of the Free Speech University Rankings.*

Notes

1. 'It Isn't Nice', by Malvina Reynolds, Malvina Reynolds: Song Lyrics and Poems, people.wku.edu/charles.smith/MALVINA/mr073.htm.
2. 'Free Speech Movement: Womens' Experience', FSM, fsm-a.org/FSM%20 Women.html.
3. Free Speech University Rankings, *spiked*, spiked-online.com/fsur.
4. Spotlight on Speech Codes 2015, FIRE, thefire.org/spotlight2015/.
5. 'Speech Codes: Alive and Well, 10 Years Later', FIRE, 15 August 2013, thefire. org/speech-codes-alive-and-well-10-years-later/.

1
From No Platform to Safe Space: A Crisis of Enlightenment

Brendan O'Neill

The academy is in crisis. On British and American campuses, a culture of intellectual caution has taken hold. Where once universities were sites of intellectual daring, spaces in which young adults could develop their understanding of the world and their moral autonomy, now they too often resemble kindergartens for grown-ups. They devote almost as much energy to protecting students from 'harmful' ideas as they do to encouraging students to open their eyes to new ways of understanding the world.

The mental robustness required for the pursuit of knowledge – for 'daring to know', as Kant aptly described the risks involved in relying on one's own reason rather than on expert revelation – is being devalued on campus. It's being replaced by a sanctification of fragility. The expectation that students have the moral and intellectual resources to deal with difficult texts, be disabused of their previous ways of thinking and take part in open-ended discussions, is giving way to a new concern for protecting their 'mental safety'.[1] Today, attendance to students' self-esteem takes precedence over the preservation of the academy as an almost sacred free space in a democratic society: the one sphere in which all claims can be tested, all ideas discussed and all intellectual possibilities entertained.

The culture of intellectual caution manifests itself in many ways. It can be seen in the rise of the 'trigger warning' phenomenon, where students demand safety notices on texts that might upset them or bring back memories of past traumatic experiences. From Ovid's *Metamorphoses* to Kant's *Critiques* ('views on race, gender, sexuality... have changed since this book was written'),[2] all sorts of intellectual works are now treated as inherently harmful, as ticking bombs of trauma. The new culture can be seen in the moral policing of classroom debate, with numerous cases on

American campuses in particular of students insisting they be given the option to avoid discussions on sensitive subject matters: race, for example, or sexual assault.[3] As a film-studies academic has complained, such a 'quest for emotional safety and psychic healing leads not to learning, but regression'.[4] And it can be seen in the frenzy for keeping off campus any thinker judged to be 'offensive' or 'hurtful'.[5] Whether it's Germaine Greer being protested against by students at Cardiff University over her alleged 'transphobia', Ayaan Hirsi Ali being denied an award from Brandeis University after students judged her to be 'Islamophobic', or far-right politicians and thinkers such as Marine Le Pen and David Irving being agitated against and even banned by students in the UK,[6] many campuses now treat controversial ways of thinking as toxic.

The fortification of the academy against offensive, insulting, 'harmful' or just different ways of thinking is best captured in the idea of the Safe Space. Sometimes, students themselves informally create Safe Space zones in which, as students at Columbia University put it, everyone must agree to 'not be oppressive in [their] interactions', or, as students at the University of Bristol in the UK insist, there must only be 'non-judgmental and non-threatening discussions'.[7] And sometimes, universities themselves declare that they are Safe Spaces, as Cardiff did in its defensive response to its students' attempts to ban Greer, when instead of defending Greer's right to speak it advertised itself as an institution which disallows 'discriminatory comments of any kind'.[8] The cultivation of spaces in which certain comments are forbidden, and where everyone must be 'non-judgemental', exposes how profound is the intellectual crisis on British and American campuses. The elevation of safety over rigorous engagement represents the death of the university as it has been understood in the modern period, as we shall see later.

The new intellectual caution impacts negatively on all the core tasks of the academy. The 'trigger warning' phenomenon, and the broader idea that 'words can wound',[9] undermines the ability of universities to encourage students to read voraciously; it calls into question John Milton's view that morally autonomous readers have 'a fundamental capacity to judge',[10] instead treating books as dangerous and students as lacking the capacity to imbibe ideas independently. The circumscribing of classroom discussion chips away at universities' ability to foster open debate through which truths might be tested and new theories arrived at. As Rani Neutill has argued, having faced student demands for classroom warnings, 'it stifles the teaching process'.[11] And the explosion in formal speech codes and conduct codes on campus, and the corresponding rise of the idea of 'microaggressions', where all sorts of innocent commentary comes to be interpreted as unwittingly racist, has shrunk the capacity of professors to engage with their students. In one notorious case, a professor at UCLA was told that his corrections of black students' grammar mistakes 'represented a form of "microaggression"'.[12] On a more day-to-day level, the ability of academics to engage frankly with their students is, as one author says, 'undermined through numerous speech codes'.[13]

So the very mission of the academy – to encourage reading of important texts, to discuss ideas with students, to judge work – is called into question by the growing culture of intellectual caution, which treats words as wounding and discussion as potentially oppressive. How did this situation come about? How has the idea of the university shifted so dramatically, from a place of autonomous thinking to a shrivelled zone of intellectual safety?

The most common explanation for this culture on campus is that a new generation that does not appreciate the importance of freedom of thought and speech is infecting university life with its prejudices. There is a growing backlash against what is being called 'the new political correctness'. Concern is growing about student self-infantilisation and the censoriousness it is nurturing. This concern can be seen among both right-wing and liberal observers, in magazine features condemning students' uber-sensitivity,[14] and even within the White House: in September 2015, President Barack Obama said students should not expect to be 'coddled and protected from different points of view'.[15]

But there is a problem with this backlash: it tends to depict the crisis on campus as a generational one. The view seems to be that millennials, being narcissistic and overly concerned with their identity, are zapping university life of its former openness and rigour. In the words of Todd Gitlin, a 'new generational norm of fragility' is undermining academic life, particularly the once-valued 'pedagogical tactic to produce discomfort'.[16] The *Nation* says students' desire to 'navigate material in a way that would be better for them psychologically' speaks to a 'generational chasm'.[17] In the UK, the *New Statesman* explicitly contrasts today's censorious students with the former generation, arguing 'undergraduates [are] rebelling against their parents' generation and its liberal deification of free speech'.[18] Even where observers recognise that university administrators play a role in cultivating the censorious culture, they generally argue that they are acquiescing to the demands of a new intolerant generation. A writer for *City Journal* says universities 'build ever-more monumental bureaucracies to indulge [the] traits' of their 'eggshell plaintiff students'.[19] The perception that the academy and its values are threatened by a new intake of debate-averse students was summed up in a remark made by an academic in a widely shared anonymous essay in 2015: 'I'm a liberal professor, and my liberal students terrify me.'[20]

This backlash is – to borrow a favoured word of today's students – 'problematic'. It de-historicises the crisis of the academy. Its treatment of this crisis as a generational turn overlooks the profound shifts in intellectual and political life that have occurred over the past 40 years and which have conspired to dent, if not destroy, the very idea of learning. The trend for mocking the moral excesses of millennial students – whether it's their branding of everyday conversation as a 'microaggression' or their fear that *The Great Gatsby* will induce PTSD among those who have experienced misogyny[21] – too often fails to take into consideration the intellectual antecedents to this climate. For what we are witnessing in the academy today is something far more serious than the arrival of a coddled generation – we're seeing the end result of the corrosion of Enlightenment values, of Western societies' abandonment of the ideals of autonomy and subjectivity upon which university life, and democratic life, have been based in the modern period. There is nothing sudden about what's happening on campus today: it has been brewing for decades, under our noses.

Liberal complacency

The current backlash against PC implicitly suggests things were largely okay on campus for the past 20 years, since the grip of the first wave of political correctness started to weaken in the early 1990s, and have only recently gone awry. In his noted essay on the return of PC, published in January 2015, Jonathan Chait claims PC had been in a 'long remission' before 'returning' in the 2010s.[22] In the UK, observers who have become concerned with students' frenzy for No Platforming controversial speakers claim this is a new development. UK students' unions have taken to No Platforming – that is, shunning from campus – everyone from radical feminists to secularists who take issue with political Islam.[23] Liberal commentators concerned about these campus bans on people they admire argue that this represents a warping of the traditional aim of No Platform, first introduced by the National Union of Students in 1974 to deal with, as the *New Statesman* puts it, 'violent fascists'.[24] A new intake of students is now restricting the 'ability to debate competing viewpoints', which is 'one of the foundations of democratic society', says the *New Statesman*.[25]

The claim that a new generation is either being uniquely censorious or is resurrecting a PC that had lain dormant for 20 years, that where the older generation practised a 'liberal deification of free speech' today's students seek only to undermine it,[26] is wrong. In fact, it speaks to one of the key problems with the rise of the new culture of intellectual caution: liberal complacency, the failure of liberal thinkers over the past four decades to challenge the growth of identity politics, intellectual relativism, and a new intolerance. For today's students only embody and express in a more upfront form ideas which have been gaining strength both on and off campus since the 1970s, often with a nod of approval from the older generation of liberals now so alarmed by what's happening to the academy.

Take the British case. The growing liberal concern with students' No Platforming posits that this policy was once narrowly designed only to prevent violence, not debate. In the words of one feminist writer, commenting on students' recent No Platforming of radical feminists, No Platform was a 'tool that was … intended to protect democracy from undemocratic movements', but it has now become 'a weapon used by the undemocratic against democracy'.[27]

This is incorrect, in two important ways. Firstly, when the UK National Union of Students (NUS) first introduced No Platform, in 1974, it wasn't only aimed at 'violent fascists'; it was explicitly 'no platform for racists and fascists' – that is, it targeted those who held prejudiced views as well as those who explicitly espoused fascistic ideas; it was aimed at thought itself, from the very start, not just 'violence'.[28] The NUS's No Platform policy enjoyed widespread support on the British left, but even here there was some debate about the inclusion of racists alongside fascists. As a writer for *Socialist Worker* asked in 1986, should No Platform really extend to 'those who simply [hold] some racist ideas', considering this would 'probably [include] the majority of trade-union members'.[29] Early on, there was a recognition that No Platform could potentially be expanded to cover other people than fascists. And secondly, and more importantly, it is wrong to present No Platform as a neat, uncontroversial policy: from the very beginning, its unwieldiness as a political weapon, its potential to generate other targets for censorship, was apparent.

Shortly after the NUS introduced No Platform, it was expanded to include Zionists. As one historical account says, 'In 1975, British students invoked the NUS resolution to disrupt speeches by Israelis and Zionists'.[30] And, ironically, the far-right National Front – a key target of the original No Platform policy – applauded this result.[31] Before long, various chapters of the Union of Jewish Students (UJS) found themselves under threat from No Platform, over their positive view of Israel. As early as 1977, a mere three years after No Platform was introduced, Alan Elsner of UJS noted its potential to be 'used as a means of silencing people whose views might be controversial or unpopular'.[32] The argument that British liberal critics now make against millennial students – that they have stretched No Platform to cover not just fascists but also controversial speakers – was in fact apparent over 35 years ago, but liberals said nothing.

In the 1980s, the remit of No Platform expanded further. It was used against the Monday Club, an anti-immigration wing of the Conservative Party, to silence Conservative MPs and ministers. In December 1986, the NUS itself felt moved to try to rein in students' unions who were using No Platform to silence Jewish, Conservative and, increasingly, Christian evangelical groups on campus. An NUS statement said: 'The abuse of this policy against those who are not declared racists or fascists brings the whole policy into disrepute.'[33] The problem was that, once the rubicon of censorship had been crossed, once the NUS had decreed that certain ideas – in the original case, fascistic ones – were too dangerous for students to hear, it was inevitable that the policy would be expanded to cover other views that students considered hurtful or threatening. This was not 'abuse' of the policy, but rather the realisation of the logic of censorship contained within it. So in the 1990s, No Platform was expanded again to cover Islamist groups such as the Muslim Public Affairs Committee and Hizb ut-Tahrir, on grounds that they're homophobic and misogynistic. After 9/11, it was extended again, so that, in the words of a student bureaucrat at the University of the West of England, 'any religious fundamentalist [is] now banned from our student union because they are seen as not compatible with a tolerant multicultural environment'.[34] Soon after, in the early 2000s, the same contradictory argument for preserving tolerance by outlawing intolerance was used to justify bans on the *Sun* newspaper and even a ban on Eminem's music at the University of Sheffield in 2001. A union official explained that 'our aim is to create a culture of tolerance, equality and respect for all our members', and 'Eminem's homophobia and misogyny spoil[s] that atmosphere'.[35] So, no equality or respect for Eminem fans.

All of this grew out of the introduction of No Platform. Once it was accepted that some ideas are too dangerous for public life, there was no reason not to apply the same principle to other ideas. The Sheffield ban on Eminem in 2001 was a significant turning point, representing student officials shifting their censorious attention from political and religious groups towards culture. Since then, the student censoring mania on British campuses has spread to include lads' magazines, allegedly sexist songs such as 'Blurred Lines', and now supposedly 'Islamophobic' or 'transphobic' feminists and leftists – that is, as Elsner predicted in 1977, people who are merely 'controversial or unpopular'.[36]

Many of those who supported No Platform are now being swallowed up by its censorious logic. The Socialist Workers' Party, which fully backed the ban on fascists, is now banned from some campuses because of its alleged 'rape apologism'. Feminists who supported restrictions on misogynistic Islamist groups now find themselves banned on the basis that they do not support transgender rights. The British liberals complaining about the out-of-control culture of intellectual caution on campus watched, uncritically, or even supportively, as this culture grew over the past 40 years. Now they only complain because they are victims of it. They clearly have not learned the first lesson of tolerance, which is that if you want your own moral views to enjoy freedom of expression then you must be fully tolerant of the expression of views you find repulsive, or 'problematic'. As John Locke argued in his *Letter Concerning Toleration*, 'What power can be given to the magistrate for the suppression of an idolatrous Church, which may not in time and place be made use of to the ruin of an orthodox one?'. Having acqui-esced to the power of students' unions to ban 'idolatrous' groups such as fascists, liberals are not in a good position now to bemoan the ruination of what they consider 'orthodox' views, such as feminism. To fortify our own freedom of speech, we must always challenge restrictions on our enemies' freedom of speech.

In the American context, the liberals concerned about the 'new political correctness' claim it represents the return, after 20 years, of a once-defeated censorious ideology. Chait argues that today's American colleges resemble 'the campus scene from two decades earlier', the last time PC was rife, before it went into 'remission'.[37] Some of the liberal critics of the 'new campus culture' point to the 1992 Supreme Court ruling against college hate-speech codes as the moment when PC in its original form was done away with. By 1992, during the first outburst of PC, more than a third of US campuses had hate-speech codes.[38] However, following various local controversies and debates, in 1992 the Supreme Court ruled, as Jon Gould describes it, that 'public institutions may not pick and choose among hateful messages when regulating speech'.[39] And so PC was defeated.

Only it wasn't. As Gould continues, by 1997, five years after the Supreme Court ruling, over half of American universities had hate-speech policies – 'a rise of nearly 30 per cent from the time of the Court's opinion'.[40] And some of these policies outlawed not only hate speech but offensive speech, too. Emory University, for example, forbade any 'oral conduct' that creates 'an offensive, demeaning, intimidating or hostile environment... [for] any person or group'.[41] In the late 1990s and 2000s, during what Chait calls the 'remission' of PC, these burgeoning codes generated a culture of censorship and numerous incidents of intolerance. In 2001, students at Brown stormed the offices of their student newspaper and seized its entire print run after it dared to publish a piece criticising reparations for slavery. In 2006, students at Dartmouth burnt copies of their newspaper after it published a cartoon that seemed to make light of date rape.[42] Such incidents led Wendy Kaminer to complain about 'the distressing number of young authoritarians on campus'.[43] Where were the liberal or left-wing critics of campus authoritarianism then? How can they now claim PC was in remission during this period when anti-offence speech codes were growing?

Not only did the number of hate-speech codes increase rather than diminish after the 1992 Supreme Court ruling, but they did so at the behest of university management itself. As Gould says, many of the codes were 'proposed and adopted by administrators, not student [activists]'.[44] So the current focus on unhinged students destroying the academy by resurrecting PC is wrong for two reasons: firstly, because PC never really went away; and second, because PC was sustained in the 1990s and 2000s as much by university management as by intolerant students.

It is hard to avoid the conclusion that, in both Britain and America, the reason liberals did not notice the continued growth of intolerance on campus in the 1980s, 1990s and 2000s is because they were not then the victims of it. The targets were right-wingers, or Islamists, or homophobes and misogynists. Having failed to challenge this censorious drive – or even worse, having been complicit in its growth – liberals cannot very well complain that they are now falling victim to the zealous crusade against 'harmful' ideas. HL Mencken argued that fighting for freedom of speech means one 'spends most of one's time defending scoundrels': 'For it is against scoundrels that oppressive laws are first aimed, and oppression must be stopped at the beginning if it is to be stopped at all.'[45] The difficulties liberals and feminists now have in speaking on campus is utterly down to their failure to defend scoundrels, to stand up for the speech rights of fascists, racists, Islamists and pornographers – not because those groups' ideas are valuable, but because when institutions assume the power to destroy moral viewpoints that are 'problematic', then it's only a matter of time before the freedom of respectable people – Locke's metaphorical 'orthodox church' – is curbed, too.

So a key contributor to the crisis of liberty on campus in the 21st century has been liberal complacency over the past 30 years. In the American case, the current situation also exposes, in a profound way, the limits to legalism when defending freedom of speech. Those who considered the problem of PC 'fixed' when the Supreme Court denounced campus speech codes in 1992 have had a rude awakening, because such codes multiplied in number and have had such an influence on the next generation that they now think little of seeking to crush anything which, echoing Emory University's 1990s code, they consider 'offensive, demeaning, intimidating'.[46] Relying on the courts to challenge worrying phenomena can leave unchallenged the extra-legal elements – the social, political and moral causes – of the crisis at hand. As Gould says, the idea that hate speech is damaging and must be regulated had gained traction across civil society, not just on campuses, in the 1980s and 1990s, which means that public debate rather than mere legal rulings was called for. He argued: 'Although the courts help to establish legal meaning with their decisions, it is just as important to win the battle in civil society by influencing the public's [view].'[47] This corrosion of the attachment to liberal values within civil society itself, beyond the walls of the university, is key to understanding the campus authoritarianism of both the 1980s and 1990s and today. Let's explore it.

The crisis of autonomy

The emergence of censorship on campus in the 1970s and 1980s – in the shape of No Platform policies in the UK and hate-speech codes in the US – did not happen in a vacuum. Rather, it was informed by huge social and political shifts in Western societies' perception of themselves and of their values and citizens. It spoke, not simply to a new intolerance among students, or a caginess about open debate among university administrators, but to a profound devaluation of the ideal of moral autonomy and its clearest everyday expression: freedom of speech.

In the UK, it wasn't an accident that students' unions started censoring hate speech in the mid- to late 1970s. The British state passed a law restricting 'incitement to racial hatred' in 1965. This criminalised 'threatening, abusive or insulting' language that was designed to 'stir up racial hatred'. The 1976 Race Relations Act went further, criminalising any 'oral or written words' that were 'threatening, abusive or insulting' to certain racial groups, even if there was no intention to stir up racial hatred. In short, simply being racist had effectively been outlawed.

Students' unions which banned anyone they judged to be 'threatening, abusive or insulting' to certain groups could claim to be acting responsibly in the eyes of the law, and they very often did. As the controversial critic of multiculturalism, Ray Honeyford, argues, the vagueness of the 1976 Act encouraged activists to 'construct highly subjective and arbitrary definitions of racism', to the extent where they can 'feel free to ban any speaker they disagree with' – the 'mentality which led to the No Platform policy of the NUS'.[48] In many ways, then, the rise of No Platform mirrored a broader legal and political shift in British society, where in the late 1960s and mid-1970s it was made an offence to make offensive racist statements.

In the US, the situation was different, because the First Amendment forbids Congress from passing laws that curb freedom of speech. And yet here, too, in the late 1970s and early 1980s, a palpable shift regarding hate speech and free speech took place. Gould describes how for much of the 20th century there had been attempts by campaigners in the US to outlaw 'group libel' speech – in essence, hate speech – and some of their efforts had been locally and temporarily successful. But for the most part, the courts asserted First Amendment rights over group protections against expressions of hatred, right up the famous Skokie case of 1978, when the US Court of Appeals for the Seventh Circuit agreed with the ACLU that even Nazis should have the right to march publicly. But a shift occurred after Skokie, says Gould. Where the 'first wave of hate-speech regulation had flamed out by the... 1970s', a 'second wave was poised to begin'.

Inspired by Title VII of the Civil Rights Act, which forbade discrimination at work on the basis of 'race, color, religion, sex or national origin', and which later came to cover 'harassment' too, a movement emerged on American campuses to outlaw 'discriminatory speech'. Similar to the emergence of anti-hate laws and campus policies in Britain in the 1970s, the speech codes that spread through American campuses after the Skokie moment of 1978 – and especially in the late 1980s and early 1990s – targeted the 'negative effects of hate messages', which can be 'real and immediate for the victims'.[49] Richard Delgado, a professor who helped to write the University of Wisconsin speech code, argued that hateful words can cause 'feelings of humiliation, isolation, and self-hatred'. Hate speech can even 'result in mental illness and psychosomatic disease' among its victims, he claimed; they may suffer 'psychological injuries'.[50] It's not hard to see where today's students get the idea that texts and words can trigger PTSD: such a dispiriting view of the dangerousness of ideas was being promoted by leaders of the academy itself more than 20 years earlier.

The codes that emerged on American campuses in the 1980s and 1990s were varied, but as Samuel Walker says they 'shared a few common elements', including the prohibition of 'demeaning forms of expression' and the protection of students from the 'hostile environment' certain forms of speech can generate.[51] The University of Connecticut went so far as to prohibit 'inappropriately directed laughter' and 'inconsiderate jokes'.[52] Walker describes how some speech-code advocates viewed 'hate speech as a form of assault' – they referred to 'assaultive racist speech'. Indeed, in the tellingly titled *Words That Wound*, published in 1993, before today's students were even born, various agitators for and authors of hate-speech codes argued that hate speech can cause 'severe psychological trauma'. They argued that black students are '*acted upon* and *constructed by* racist speech' (my italics).[53] Here, words are imbued with an extraordinary physical power, and by the same token the hearer of words is denuded of his autonomy entirely, of his ability to reject, engage with or challenge speech; rather, he is casually, inevitably 'acted upon' by speech.[54]

This view of speech as a threat to allegedly vulnerable minority students very often came from the heart of the academy. As Walker says, 'The role of law professors was critical': they helped draft speech codes and also wrote publicly in defence of them.[55] What's more, 'with few exceptions, university administrators were receptive to [the] proposed codes'.[56] And thus did professors and administrators themselves push the idea of speech as psychologically traumatic, as 'assaultive', more than two decades ago.

If these arguments that were being made by leading academics post-Skokie, post-1978, sound familiar, that's because they are the antecedents of what we have on campus today. Liberal observers mock students' talk of 'microaggressions', but this is merely an expansion of the older idea of 'assaultive speech'. They ridicule students who claim certain books may cause them trauma, but how is this different to the arguments of those sections of the academy which 20 years ago were presenting racist speech as 'psychologically traumatic'? We criticise students' cultivation of Safe Spaces, but these are surely only the corollary of old speech codes claiming that certain forms of speech create 'hostile environments'. The Safe Space is the solution to the Western academy's own, self-defeating reduction of itself to the level of a 'hostile environment'.

It is telling that it was in the late 1970s and early 1980s, in both Britain and America, that a new and censorious concern with hate speech emerged. What we really witnessed back then was a rethinking of the idea of the individual himself and his ability to exercise moral agency and judgement in the public sphere of discussion. As a result of various historical shifts, towards the end of the 20th century, especially following the tumultuous decade of capitalist uncertainty and questioning of progress that was the 1970s, the old Millian view of the robust individual began to wither. We saw the corrosion of the Enlightenment view of individuals as capable of self-government, where, in John Stuart Mill's words, the individual uses 'observation to see, reasoning and judgement to foresee, activity to gather materials for decision, discrimination to decide, and when he has decided, firmness and self-control to hold to his deliberate decision'.[57] In contrast, from the 1970s onwards, and most strikingly in the academy, we've seen the emergence of a view of the individual as 'acted upon' by speech, traumatised by ideas and lacking the firmness even to be able to read a book without therapeutic guidance.

In essence, the throttling of freedom of speech on campus speaks to the late 20th-century diminution of the ideal of autonomy. C Edwin Baker, author of *Human Liberty and Freedom of Speech* (1989), argued that freedom of speech is the most important outward expression, and guarantee, of the autonomy of the individual: 'The key ethical postulate is that respect for individual integrity and autonomy requires the recognition that a person has the right to use speech to develop herself or to influence or interact with others in a manner that corresponds to her values.'[58] Nadine Strossen recognised the fundamental nature of what was at stake in the campus controversies of the past 30 years: the idea that individuals have 'the critical capacity to evaluate and reject ideas'.[59] There is far more to the 30-year rise of a culture of intellectual caution than the restriction of certain individuals' right to express themselves; the moral capacity of all students, and by extension all adults, has been called into question. That is, the idea of moral autonomy itself was traduced, and the keenest expression of this undermining of autonomy was the depiction of speech as dangerous, as assault.

The traditional ideal of autonomy treated individuals as capable of both understanding and impacting on the world. The new view of humanity sees us as lacking the capacity to judge ideas and as being unwittingly 'acted upon' by the world, or just by words. The post-Renaissance ideal of human subjectivity – which viewed individuals as capable of shaping their fate and their surroundings by 'the many operations of intelligence and will'[60] – has given way to a view of humans as mere objects: as shaped, not shaper. Words 'construct us'.[61] The contemporary questioning of human subjectivity itself is keenly felt on campus. Alongside restraints on speech, we have seen the rise over the past 30 years of therapeutic interventions designed to alleviate students' alleged mental stress, homesickness and general feelings of malaise. This has contributed to the infantilisation of the student body, which grates against the very notion of learning. As Joanna Williams has argued: 'In order to exercise subjectivity, students must have some sense of themselves as actors or "agents" in the world: resilient in the face of change, capable of influencing their environment... With a diminished sense of their subjectivity, students may not have such a firm belief in themselves as resilient, capable actors, and instead might see themselves as vulnerable, fragile and in need of support.'[62]

This is the situation we find ourselves in now: with an academy inhabited by students who have an extremely underwritten sense of subjectivity, not because they are inherently weak but because they have been schooled in institutions which for more than 30 years have restricted speech, diminished autonomy, redefined ideas as hurtful and actively incited the cultivation of a vulnerable personality which sees learning as a form of abuse.

The ideology of safety

The corrosion of the ideal of autonomy has impacted on all areas of the human experience. It has led to increased state intervention into our personal lives at the level of health, parenting and domestic relationships. It has led to an explosion in a new class of experts keen to advise us on everything from how to have sex to what we should eat. And it has generated new laws, or informal systems of self-censorship, which control what we may express, or what we think we should express. If the birth of Enlightenment represented, in Kant's words, a desire to break free of those who 'set themselves up as guardians' and to 'walk firmly and cultivate [one's] own mind', then today's anti-Enlightenment undermining of autonomy has created vast new industries of 'guardians', which are determined to protect us from harmful speech, hurtful people, interpersonal relationships and life in general.

But the assault on autonomy has impacted most profoundly on the academy. There, it has caused a crisis of mission of epic proportions. Why? Because the university is fundamentally built on the ideal of autonomy, and on the practice of human subjectivity. It is predicated on a view of students as capable of intellectual engagement, and of impacting on others and the world itself through their ideas and their speech. When autonomy and subjectivity are demoted, as they are today, then the university itself becomes an impossibility. It becomes transformed from an open intellectual space into a Safe Space; from a zone in which ideas are shared and judged to a place where ideas are feared and viewed as 'psychologically traumatic'; from an institution in which students are encouraged to act on others through their speech to one where the fear of being 'acted upon' leads to the shutting down of discussion. A university that becomes a Safe Space destroys itself.

The ideology of 'safety' on the 21st-century campus is striking. It speaks, profoundly, to the intellectual stasis of our era. Since the Renaissance and the Enlightenment, thinkers have emphasised the risks inherent in discovery and intellectual curiosity. It is possible for individuals to reach the 'highest pinnacle of glory', said the 15th-century Italian scholar Leon Battista Alberti, even though 'invidious Fortune opposes us'. 'Dare to know!', cried Kant. Mill encouraged us to allow everyone 'the liberty of contradicting and disproving our opinion', however hurtful such an experience might be, in order that we might grow intellectually. All emphasised taking risks. Now, the watchword is 'safety'. It's a codeword for hiding away, retreating from our human responsibility to study, discover and debate in order that we might expand the pool of human knowledge and improve human life. The Safe Space is a trap, granting students temporal comfort at the expense of allowing them to use their mental and moral muscles both to understand and to change the world. Ending the Safe Space will require more than critiques of the young – it demands a serious, far-reaching intellectual effort to repair the fraying ideals of freedom, autonomy and the Enlightenment itself.

Brendan O'Neill *is editor of* spiked.

Notes

1. 'Free speech is so last century. Today's students want the "right to be comfortable"', by Brendan O'Neill, *Spectator*, 22 November 2014, spectator.co.uk/2014/11/free-speech-is-so-last-century-todays-students-want-the-right-to-be-comfortable/.
2. 'Life is triggering. The best literature should be, too', by Jerry A Coyne, *New Republic*, 14 May 2015, newrepublic.com/article/121790/life-triggering-best-literature-should-be-too.
3. 'My trigger warning disaster', by Rani Neutill, *Salon*, 28 October 2015, salon.com/2015/10/28/i_wanted_to_be_a_supporter_of_survivors_on_campus_and_a_good_teacher_i_didnt_realize_just_how_impossible_this_would_be/.
4. 'My trigger warning disaster', salon.com/2015/10/28/i_wanted_to_be_a_supporter_of_survivors_on_campus_and_a_good_teacher_i_didnt_realize_just_how_impossible_this_would_be/.
5. 'Trouble on campus: the rise of ban-happy student leaders', by Brendan O'Neill, *Sunday Telegraph*, 1 November 2015, telegraph.co.uk/education/

universityeducation/11658770/Trouble-on-campus-the-rise-of-ban-happy-student-leaders.html.

6. 'French far-right leader Marine Le Pen mobbed by Oxford Union protesters', by Gregory Walton, *Daily Telegraph*, 5 February 2015, telegraph.co.uk/news/worldnews/europe/france/11394170/French-far-right-leader-Marine-Le-Pen-mobbed-by-Oxford-Union-protesters.html.

7. 'If you don't want to debate rape or racism, you shouldn't have come to Uni', by Gabriel Dorey, *Tab*, 13 November 2014, thetab.com/uk/bristol/2014/11/13/dont-want-debate-rape-racism-shouldnt-come-uni-12127.

8. 'Petition urges Cardiff University to cancel Germaine Greer lecture', by Ben Quinn, *Guardian*, 23 October 2015, theguardian.com/education/2015/oct/23/petition-urges-cardiff-university-to-cancel-germain-greer-lecture.

9. *Words That Wound: Critical Race Theory, Assaultive Speech and the First Amendment*, by Mari J Matsuda et al., Westview Press, 1993.

10. *Power of Reading: From Socrates to Twitter*, by Frank Furedi, Bloomsbury, 2015

11. 'My trigger warning disaster', salon.com/2015/10/28/i_wanted_to_be_a_supporter_of_survivors_on_campus_and_a_good_teacher_i_didnt_realize_just_how_impossible_this_would_be/.

12. 'In-class sit-in', by Colleen Flaherty, *Inside Higher Ed*, 25 November 2013, insidehighered.com/news/2013/11/25/ucla-grad-students-stage-sit-during-class-protest-what-they-see-racially-hostile.

13. 'Dissent? Not today, thank you', by Frank Furedi, *Times Higher Education Supplement*, 9 September 2005.

14. 'Not a very PC thing to say', by Jonathan Chait, *New York Magazine*, 27 January 2015, nymag.com/daily/intelligencer/2015/01/not-a-very-pc-thing-to-say.html.

15. 'Obama says liberal college students should not be "coddled"', by Janell Ross, *Washington Post*, 15 September 2015, washingtonpost.com/news/the-fix/wp/2015/09/15/obama-says-liberal-college-students-should-not-be-coddled-are-we-really-surprised/.

16. 'Why you should be disturbed at college', by Todd Gitlin, *Tablet*, 13 March 2015, tabletmag.com/jewish-news-and-politics/189543/trigger-warnings-on-campus.

17. 'The Laura Kipnis Melodrama', by Michelle Goldberg, *Nation*, 16 March 2015, thenation.com/article/laura-kipnis-melodrama/.

18. 'What the row over banning Germaine Greer is really about', by Helen Lewis, *New Statesman*, 27 October 2015, newstatesman.com/politics/feminism/2015/10/what-row-over-banning-germaine-greer-really-about.

19. 'The Microaggression Farce', by Heather MacDonald, *City Journal*, Autumn 2014, city-journal.org/mobile/story.php?s=10764#.Vje4ol50Wrc.

20. 'I'm a liberal professor, and my liberal students terrify me', by Edward Schlosser, *Vox*, 3 June 2015, vox.com/2015/6/3/8706323/college-professor-afraid

21. 'US students request trigger warnings on literature', by Alison Flood, *Guardian*, 19 May 2014, theguardian.com/books/2014/may/19/us-students-request-trigger-warnings-in-literature.

22. 'Not a very PC thing to say', nymag.com/daily/intelligencer/2015/01/not-a-very-pc-thing-to-say.html.

23. 'Student union blocks speech by "inflammatory" anti-sharia activist', by Richard Adams, *Guardian*, 26 September 2015, theguardian.com/education/2015/sep/26/student-union-blocks-speech-activist-maryam-namazie-warwick.

24. '"No platform" was once reserved for violent fascists. Now it's being used to silence debate', by Sarah Ditum, *New Statesman*, 18 March 2014, newstatesman.com/sarah-ditum/2014/03/when-did-no-platform-become-about-attacking-individuals-deemed-disagreeable.
25. '"No platform" was once reserved for violent fascists', newstatesman.com/sarah-ditum/2014/03/when-did-no-platform-become-about-attacking-individuals-deemed-disagreeable.
26. 'What the row over banning Germaine Greer is really about', newstatesman.com/politics/feminism/2015/10/what-row-over-banning-germaine-greer-really-about.
27. '"No platform" was once reserved for violent fascists', newstatesman.com/sarah-ditum/2014/03/when-did-no-platform-become-about-attacking-individuals-deemed-disagreeable.
28. 'No Platform: free speech for all?', by Lindsey German, *Socialist Worker Review*, April 1986.
29. 'No Platform: free speech for all?'.
30. *Litigating Rights: Perspectives from Domestic and International Law*, by Grant Huscroft and Paul Rishworth (eds), Hart, 2002.
31. *Litigating Rights*.
32. 'What's new about No Platform mania?', by Mick Hume, *spiked*, 8 October 2015, spiked-online.com/newsite/article/17526#.Vje_Q150Wrc.
33. 'Who gets the platform?', by Francis Beckett, *New Statesman*, 5 December 1986.
34. 'The "No Platform" issue returns to campus', by Johann Hari, *New Statesman*, 9 December 2002, newstatesman.com/node/194576.
.35. 'Students revolt as union bans Eminem', by Angelique Chrisafis, *Guardian*, 2 February 2001.
36. 'What's new about No Platform mania?', spiked-online.com/newsite/article/17526#.Vje_Q150Wrc.
37. 'Not a very PC thing to say', nymag.com/daily/intelligencer/2015/01/not-a-very-pc-thing-to-say.html.
38. *Speak No Evil: The Triumph of Hate Speech Regulation*, by Jon Gould, University of Chicago Press, 2005.
39. *Speak No Evil*.
40. *Speak No Evil*.
41. *Speak No Evil*.
42. 'Students are supposed to read books, not burn them', by Brendan O'Neill, *spiked*, 18 November 2010, spiked-online.com/newsite/article/9905#.VjfEsF50Wrc.
43. 'The left has been infected by the disease of intolerance', Interview with Wendy Kaminer, *spiked*, 27 October 2006, spiked-online.com/newsite/article/2031#.VjfFA150Wrc.
44. *Speak No Evil*.
45. *Collected Works of HL Mencken*, Kindle Edition, 17 February 2014.
46. *Speak No Evil*.
47. *Speak No Evil*.
48. *The Commission for Racial Equality: British Bureaucracy and the Multiethnic Society*, by Ray Honeyford, Transaction, 1998.
49. *Words That Wound*.

50. *Words That Wound.*
51. *Hate Speech: The History of an American Controversy,* by Samuel Walker, University of Nebraska Press, 1994.
52. *Hate Speech.*
53. *Words That Wound.*
54. *Words That Wound.*
55. *Hate Speech.*
56. *Hate Speech.*
57. *On Liberty,* by John Stuart Mill, 1859, bartleby.com/130/.
58. *Human Liberty and Freedom of Speech,* by C Edwin Baker, Oxford University Press, 1989.
59. *Hate Speech Law: A Philosophical Explanation,* by Alex Brown, Routledge, 2015.
60. *The Foundation of Modern Political Thought,* by Quentin Skinner, Cambridge University Press, 1978.
61. *Words That Wound.*
62. *The Marketisation of Higher Education,* Molesworth et al. (eds), Routledge, 2011.

2

The 'New' Feminism and the Fear of Free Speech

Nancy McDermott

In November 2014, a student group called Oxford Students For Life invited journalists Brendan O'Neill and Tim Stanley to Christ Church College, Oxford to debate the proposition 'This House Believes Britain's Abortion Culture Hurts Us All'. But no sooner was the event advertised on Facebook than a group of around 300 students set up a rival page railing against the prospect of men debating abortion. According to the protesters, the debate was bound to feature 'really shitty anti-choice rhetoric and probs [sic] cis-sexism',[1] and would threaten the 'mental safety' of Oxford students.[2] They invited their fellow undergraduates to bring 'non-destructive but oh-so-disruptive instruments' to shut down the event. The Oxford University Students' Union Women's Campaign (WomCam) quickly jumped on the bandwagon, condemning Oxford Students For Life for holding an event in which 'two cis-gender men debate about what people with uteruses should be doing with their bodies'.[3]

In another time and place, students might have been enthusiastic about a debate on a topic they felt strongly about, and most would have turned up on the night to support their side regardless of who was speaking. But not in the Oxford of 2014. Christ Church cancelled the event in short order due to 'potential security and welfare issues'.[4]

The abortion debate that never happened is a good place to start a discussion about feminism and free speech on university campuses today. Not only are feminists at the forefront of the campaign to shut down speech in Oxford and elsewhere, but the ideas of victimhood and vulnerability, so often associated with modern-day feminism, have come to dominate the cultural and intellectual life of the academy.

In what we'll see is a recurring theme on campuses today, the students who shut down the Oxford abortion debate expressed an exaggerated sense of fragility, coupled with a sense of entitlement; they felt within their rights to shut down speech they disliked with impunity, while simultaneously claiming they were not censoring anyone. As Niamh McIntyre, one of the organisers of the Facebook protest group, bragged in the *Independent*: 'I did not stifle free speech. As a student I asserted that it would make me feel threatened at my own university.'[5]

In the following chapter, I'll look more closely at some recent feminist-led attacks on free expression on British and American campuses, identify the continuities these attacks had with feminist ideas of the 1980s and 1990s, and look at the factors that have led to their seeming resurgence over the past few years.

Title IX and sexual harassment

Laura Kipnis is a self-described feminist and professor of communication studies at Northwestern University. In February 2015, she wrote an article for the *Chronicle of Higher Education* challenging a new Northwestern policy she believed represented a dialling back of a lot of the progress women have made in establishing themselves as consenting adults: the prohibition of students and faculty dating one another.[6]

Within days of the publication of 'Sexual Paranoia Strikes Academe', Kipnis found herself at the centre of a storm. Facebook and Twitter users were outraged by 'the violence expressed by her message'. Feminists on campus started a petition urging Northwestern to issue a 'swift, official condemnation' of her article and staged protests carrying mattresses and pillows – a method of protesting against perceived injustice in campus sexual-assault proceedings popularised by a Columbia University student known as 'mattress girl'.[7]

If all this were not enough, Kipnis soon learned that two students, both women, had lodged complaints against her under Title IX, the federal law that prohibits sex discrimination in schools that receive federal funding. One claimed she was lodging her complaint 'on behalf of the university community', alleging that Kipnis's essay had a 'chilling effect' on the ability of students to report sexual misconduct. The other complainant claimed that Kipnis was retaliating against her because her essay made a passing reference (without mentioning any names or specific details) to a legal case she was involved in. Because Title IX complaints are a matter of civil rights the university was obliged to engage a special legal team to carry out an investigation.

Even though the complaints were eventually dismissed, Kipnis endured a 72-day-long, Kafkaesque investigation, during which she was not entitled to legal representation, or to know the charges, or the evidence, being presented against her in advance. Writing about her ordeal, she lamented:

> You can mock academic culture all you want, and I've done a fair amount of it myself, but I also believe that unconstrained intellectual debate – once the ideal of university life, now on life support – is essential to a functioning democratic society. And that should concern us all. I also find it depressing to witness young women on campuses – including aspiring intellectuals! – trying to induce university powers to shield them from the umbrages of life and calling it feminism.[8]

Kipnis's ordeal highlighted two of the most important features of recent attacks on free speech and academic freedom in the US. The first is a blurring of the line between speech and harmful actions, and the second is the institutionalisation of this confusion through sexual-harassment protocol.

Title IX was intended to stop gender-based discrimination in education – equal provisions for sports facilities, in the first instance – but the Obama administration has used it to try to address the problem of sexual harassment and sexual assault. In May 2013, in a joint letter to the University of Montana concerning its mishandling of sexual-assault allegations, the Department of Education and the Department of Justice rewrote the definition of sexual harassment to include 'unwelcome conduct of a sexual nature', including 'verbal conduct', even if an objective 'reasonable person' of the same gender does not find it threatening.[9] Not only is this definition entirely subjective, it effectively negates freedom of speech by collapsing the distinction between words and actions. And a similar process has taken place in the UK, with the National Union of Students (NUS) promoting zero-tolerance policies for sexual harassment that cover merely offensive sexual speech.[10]

As Kipnis found out, the official redefinition of sexual harassment has fuelled feminist campaigns to shut down speech on campus.

According to *spiked*'s 2015 Free Speech University Rankings, 80 per cent of UK universities – including university administrations and students' unions – censor speech to some degree, and 41 per cent mandate explicit restrictions on certain ideas, ideologies, political affiliations, beliefs, books, speakers and words. The vast majority of bans the *spiked* survey uncovered, including the banning of Robin Thicke's 'Blurred Lines' at 21 universities and the banning of the *Sun* newspaper at 26 universities (because of the topless models on Page 3), are the direct result of feminist campaigns.[11]

A similar study in the United States by the Foundation for Individual Rights in Education found that 55 per cent of colleges reviewed had at least one policy that clearly and substantially restricted free speech. A further 39 per cent had speech policies so vague that offensive or challenging ideas could be treated in the same way as threats, violence and harassment, lest they fall foul of Title IX regulations.[12]

Perhaps unsurprisingly, this institutionalisation of restrictions on speech has reinforced the idea that speech can pose a danger to students, and female students in particular. This has helped to create an expectation that campus authorities should intervene in all aspects of student life, not just academic matters, and censor offensive content in order to protect vulnerable students.

Regulating 'pulling'

Dapper Laughs, star of a now-cancelled UK TV show called *Dapper Laughs: On the Pull*, is, in a word, awful. He is rude, arrogant, sexist and obnoxious. He yells at women from his car, calling them 'gash' – a slang word for vagina – and offers up cringe-making advice to men in his audience about how to 'pull birds'. He is also a fictional character, a parody of British 'lad culture' created by comedian Daniel O'Reilly. He is intended as a cautionary tale, not a role model. As O'Reilly later told BBC's *Newsnight*: 'I thought that the people that were viewing it were saying "this is ridiculous" and laughing at it.'[13]

Not everyone got the joke. In November 2014, O'Reilly's upcoming performance at Cardiff University was called off after feminist students launched a petition claiming his jokes 'centre around the trivialisation of rape, unprotected sex and dehumanising women'.[14] The gig was cancelled, and in the ensuing controversy ITV2 declined to renew his show for another season.

Like the Oxford feminists who forced the cancellation of the abortion debate, the petition's organiser denied she was censoring him. 'Dapper Laughs can go and play in any external venue he wants, but it's not appropriate in an academic venue where it goes against our policies.' If anything, she suggested the ban was a positive move for free speech, as it 'started a talk about feminism and sexism on campus'.[15]

The policy that the Dapper Laughs gig went against was Cardiff University Students' Union's 'Anti-Lad Culture Policy', adopted as part of an NUS initiative to tackle lad culture. Lad culture, like its American counterpart frat culture, is described by the NUS as 'a "pack" mentality resulting in "banter" that is often sexist, misogynistic and homophobic. Heavy alcohol consumption is often involved. It is a sexualised culture that often involves the objectification of women and rape-supportive attitudes.'[16] But the main problem, according to the NUS, is that it 'detracts from the idea of the university as a community of young people with shared values such as equality, social justice and mutual support'.[17]

As part of its anti-lad-culture initiatives, the NUS has encouraged students around the country to ban newspapers, magazines and sexist songs, and to work with colleges to institute consent workshops, gender-equity training (with sports clubs especially) and awareness training for all members of staff.

In reality, it is hard to distinguish 'lad culture' from the hyper-sexualised, sometimes ludicrous interactions between immature students that have always been part of college life. Many women willingly participate in 'lad culture',[18] and though some feel uncomfortable with it, most women interviewed in an NUS study about the impact of lad culture did not feel it had directly affected their studies, and had the 'overall sense that universities were positive academic environments for women'.[19] But, as we will see in our next example, the possibility of causing discomfort for some has become reason enough for campus feminists to consider banning it for all.

Feeling uncomfortable

Wellesley is a prestigious women-only liberal-arts college just west of Boston. It is known for its academics and counts Hillary Clinton and Madeleine Albright among its alumni. In February 2014, the college's Davis Museum put on *New Gravity*, a solo show by artist Tony Matelli. The exhibition featured playful, hyperrealistic sculptures: a vase of fresh flowers suspended upside down in mid-air; ropes climbing up to knot themselves; a young man floating just above the floor of the gallery. And two sculptures, 'Stray Dog', a solitary guide dog in a harness, and 'Sleepwalker', a somnambulating man in his underwear, were installed outside the museum on the campus grounds.

Within a few days of the opening, a petition appeared on Change. org demanding that 'Sleepwalker' be removed because it was 'a source of apprehension, fear and triggering thoughts regarding sexual assault for some members of our campus community'.[20] Lisa Fischman, the museum's director, responded with a letter defending the work and asserting that 'art provokes dialogue, and discourse is the core of education'. But if Fischman hoped the controversy might lead to a discussion of art, she was badly mistaken. Angry petitioners dismissed her response as 'self-serving and inadequate'. After all, they weren't focused on the work itself; they were much more focused on the perilous state of students' emotions.

'Wellesley should be "a safe place" for students, not a triggering one', wrote one young woman in a comment under the petition. Another declared, 'We shouldn't be subjected to something that makes us uncomfortable. Wellesley is supposed to be our home. How dare you take that sense of safety and ease away from your students?' These students repeatedly emphasised the need for a Safe Space and their 'right' not to be made to feel uncomfortable.

Not all Wellesley students felt unsafe – some stopped to take selfies with the sculpture, to brush snow off his nose or to dress him in scarves and hats, more in keeping with the unusually cold winter – but very few were prepared to defend the work or its placement. Both the sculpture's supporters and detractors accepted that a subsection of women would be upset by the sculpture and felt it was the job of the college to protect them.

'Do people not understand what it means to be a woman in our society?', asked one of the signatories to the petition. 'To walk back from an evening class with the thought at the back of your mind that you may not reach home because a fellow student or a passerby – stronger, larger – might decide for you that you're not going to reach home?'

Though the college ultimately chose not to remove the sculpture, in a statement Wellesley president Kim Bottomly emphasised 'we must do everything we can to support those students who find themselves affected by it'.[21]

Trigger warnings

Perhaps the most interesting emergent trend in the regulation of speech on campus today are campaigns for trigger warnings. Trigger warnings are content warnings or disclaimers which are placed on books, articles or other materials to warn readers about references to anything that might prove upsetting, or 'triggering', to particular people – specifically people who may have suffered trauma. But the long list of content they cover, ranging from sexual abuse to merely sexism, reflect that they have begun to cover ideas or speech which are merely upsetting or offensive.

Trigger warnings first appeared on internet forums as a way of moderating discussion for trauma victims or the mentally ill. They migrated to the feminist blogosphere and then into academia, where some instructors added them to course materials to oblige particular students.[22] More recently, however, calls for mandatory trigger warnings have gained momentum. In 2014, students at the University of California, Rutgers University and Columbia University made headlines when they demanded professors use trigger warnings on books including F Scott Fitzgerald's *The Great Gatsby* and Ovid's *Metamorphoses*. Though trigger warnings are mainly a US phenomenon, they are beginning to appear informally on course materials in UK universities.

If we accept the model of the university as a Safe Space or a 'supportive community' on the one hand, and the idea of the fragility of students on the other, trigger warnings make perfect sense. But they also make educating students very difficult. In a piece for the *New Yorker* in December 2014, Harvard law professor Jeannie Suk noted that 'student organisations representing women's interests now routinely advise students that they should not feel pressured to attend or participate in class sessions that focus on the law of sexual violence, and which might therefore be traumatic'.[23]

If professors continue to teach topics like rape law in the depth and detail they deserve, students may decline to take part. But, if professors mark students down because they have not mastered the material, they may be accused of discrimination. 'Even seasoned teachers of criminal law, at law schools across the country, have confided that they are seriously considering dropping rape law and other topics related to sex and gender violence', wrote Suk. The ultimate irony of feminist campaigns to protect students from the discomfort of talking about sexual violence may be the loss of a generation of professionals capable of helping those women who actually experience it.

A 'new' feminism?

At the moment, it is members of the older generation, many of them feminists themselves, who are most concerned about censorious developments on college campuses. Many older feminists have presented the rise of feminist censorship as a generational shift. Kipnis points to the rise of helicopter parenting as an influence on this new, censorious generation, while British feminist Julie Bindel, who has been officially No Platformed by the NUS due to her views on transgenderism, also points to young people's comfortable upbringing: '[They are] so obsessed with their own privileged upbringing, their own privileged status, that they think they are literally accessing a commercial service at university ... They're just pampered and they think everything should go their way.'[24]

However, while there is clearly a generational element to current developments, campus-feminist censorship today is still very much informed by the so-called third-wave feminism of the 1980s and 1990s.

The history of feminism as a social and political movement is usually described as falling into three distinct historical phases, or 'waves'. First-wave feminism refers to the movement for women's equality that grew out of the European Enlightenment and culminated in the women's suffrage movement in the early part of the 20th century. It is associated with figures like Mary Wollstonecraft and the Suffragettes in the UK, and Susan B Anthony and Elizabeth Cady Stanton in the US.

Second-wave feminism, sometimes called 'the women's liberation movement', began in the 1950s and lasted roughly up to 1980. These feminists focused on abolishing inequalities in law and in custom. They campaigned for equal pay, equal opportunities in the job market, and the right to contraception and abortion. Second-wave feminism produced a large number of writers and thinkers, such as Germaine Greer, Simone de Beauvoir and Betty Friedan, whose book *The Feminine Mystique* is usually credited with sparking the birth of the new women's movement.

Third-wave feminism arose in the 1980s and lasted into the 1990s. By the end of the 1970s, most formal inequalities between men and women were gone or going, and young people took it as self-evident that women were just as capable as men. With so many of the old barriers fallen, feminism became a movement in search of a cause. Influenced by postmodernism, third-wave feminists began to shift their focus from democratic reforms towards the family, culture, language and constructions of gender. The slogan 'the personal is political' came to define a movement that organised itself around lifestyle and identity.

Two 1980s figures, writer Andrea Dworkin and legal scholar Catharine MacKinnon, arguably did the most to lay the basis for contemporary feminism. Both identified pornography as the vehicle through which men enforce their power over women. Not only were the words and images of pornography sometimes the products of sexual exploitation and violence – inflicted upon the women involved – but their mere existence caused actual harm to women. MacKinnon and Dworkin lobbied for pornography to be banned by the government, on the basis that it undermined equality. 'There is no requirement that the state remain neutral between equality and inequality', MacKinnon wrote in her 1993 book *Only Words*. 'Equality is a compelling state interest that can already outweigh First Amendment rights in certain settings.'[25]

In contrast to second-wave feminists who experienced state regulations as a barrier to their equality – particularly in terms of abortion and contraception – third-wave feminists saw state regulation as a necessary precondition of it. The underlying assumption was that the forces of patriarchy are naturally brutalising to women to the extent that they can't possibly overcome it on their own. In other words, women are inherently vulnerable, and need the authorities to intervene in order to save them from male domination – which is often not physical or structural, but based in language and cultural norms. When campus feminists today call for women to be protected from laddish humour, when they say women are made to feel 'unsafe' by studying rape law or looking at a campus sculpture, they are echoing these very sentiments.

The rise of feminism, the decline of democracy

The ideas of third-wave feminism have always been broadly unpopular. Polls though the 1990s and into the 2000s showed a steady decrease in the numbers of women who identified themselves as feminists; in at least one poll, carried out by *Time* and CNN, 40 per cent of women actually expressed hostility to feminism.[26] For a long time, the influence of third-wave feminism seemed confined to pockets in academia, NGOs and non-profits, and was largely ignored by the majority of people.

What then explains the apparent resurgence of feminism on campus today? There is no great demand for feminism in Western society at large. Indeed, women have made great strides in a remarkably short time. On both sides of the Atlantic, women outnumber men in higher education and outperform them academically.[27] Young women earn the same or more than young men,[28] and rates of domestic violence have fallen in the US[29] and the UK.[30] And, in the United States, women are just as likely to be the perpetrators of domestic abuse as men.[31] It is only when women start families that their pay and opportunities decline relative to men[32] – but even there progress is being made.[33]

Feminism remains deeply unpopular. Polls in Britain[34] and the US[35] show that the vast majority of men and women who believe in equal rights reject the feminist label. And though feminist researchers are eager to point out that women under 30 are more likely to embrace the label today than in the past, feminists make up only a very narrow section of society. More importantly, feminism represents something different to young women today than in earlier periods. It is understood less as a movement with clear-cut political goals, than as a species of identity expressing a particular set of values.

The rise of feminism on university campuses probably has less to do with feminism and more to do with the changing context in which feminists operate. The message that women are inherently vulnerable because of male-dominated culture resonates strongly with students who have been raised to prize emotion over objectivity and sensitivity over resilience, and who arrive at university to find vast swathes of speech censored for the sake of protecting their 'mental wellbeing'.

Feminism has merely profited from the degradation of liberal principles, on campus and elsewhere; feminism is, as Brendan O'Neill has described, 'the gloss on Western society's own collapse of faith in itself'.[36] Western society is no longer able to uphold the universal values that once provided a positive moral vision for the future. As a movement beholden to identity politics, feminism cannot provide an alternative universalising vision. But it can serve as an alternative source of direction and moral authority, given women's position as the oldest and most enduring 'Other'. At a time of competitive identities, in which different groups jostle for victimised status, feminism provides a fragile, pluralist connection between disparate groups.

This is why governments, educational institutions and politicians are so keen to make feminists' concerns their own. But what officialdom gains from backing campus feminism comes at the price of creating a generation of adults too emotionally fragile to develop ideas or meet the challenge of running a complex society. For people who still have faith in the capacity of students to cope with adversity, and to thrive in a challenging environment, opposing campus feminism and defending free expression on campus are vital. Not just for students to live up to their academic potential, but for the future of democracy itself.

Nancy McDermott is a writer based in New York.

Notes

1. 'Oxford students shut down abortion debate. Free speech is under assault on campus', by Tim Stanley, *Telegraph*, 19 November 2014, telegraph.co.uk/news/politics/11239437/Oxford-students-shut-down-abortion-debate.-Free-speech-is-under-assault-on-campus.html.
2. 'Free speech is so last century. Today's Students Want the "Right To Be Comfortable"', by Brendan O'Neill, *Spectator*, 22 November 2014, spectator.co.uk/features/9376232/free-speech-is-so-last-century-todays-students-want-the-right-to-be-comfortable/.

3. '"Abortion culture" debate provokes student outrage', *Oxford Student*, 27 November 2014, oxfordstudent.com/2014/11/17/abortion-culture-debate-provokes-student-outrage/.
4. 'Christ Church refuses to hold "Abortion Culture" Debate', *Cherwell*, 17 November 2014, cherwell.org/news/college/2014/11/17/christ-church-refuses-to-hold-quotabortion-culturequot-debate.
5. 'I helped shut down an abortion debate between two men because my uterus isn't up for their discussion', by Niamh McIntyre, *Independent*, 18 November 2014, independent.co.uk/voices/comment/i-helped-shut-down-an-abortion-debate-between-two-men-because-my-uterus-isnt-up-for-their-discussion-9867200.html.
6. 'Sexual Paranoia Strikes Academe', by Laura Kipnis, *Chronicle of Higher Education*, 27 February 2015, chronicle.com/article/Sexual-Paranoia/190351/.
7. 'The Laura Kipnis Melodrama', by Michelle Goldberg, *Nation*, 16 March 2015, thenation.com/article/laura-kipnis-melodrama/.
8. 'My Title IX Inquisition', by Laura Kipnis, *Chronicle of Higher Education*, 29 May 2015, chronicle.com/article/My-Title-IX-Inquisition/230489/.
9. 'Departments of Education and Justice: National "Blueprint" for Unconstitutional Speech Codes', FIRE, thefire.org/cases/departments-of-education-and-justice-national-requirement-for-unconstitutional-speech-codes/.
10. 'Becoming a Zero Tolerance Union: Ending sexual harassment in your union', National Union of Students, nusu.co.uk/pageassets/yourunion/documents/a-z/zero-tolerance-sexual-harrassment-policy-nus.pdf.
11. Free Speech University Rankings, February 2015, spiked-online.com/fsur.
12. 'Spotlight on Speech Codes 2015', FIRE, thefire.org/spotlight-speech-codes-2015/.
13. '"Dapper Laughs Is Gone" WARNING: OFFENSIVE LANGUAGE – Daniel O'Reilly – Newsnight', YouTube, 11 November 2014, youtube.com/watch?v=lBt3fr5viAE.
14. 'Ban Dapper Laughs' Show', by Vicky Chandler, Change.org, change.org/p/cardiff-university-students-union-ban-dapper-laughs-show?recruiter=25628497&utm_campaign=twitter_link_action_box&utm_medium=twitter&utm_source=share_petition#petition-letter.
15. 'Cardiff University Students' Union cancels gig by "sexist" Dapper Laughs after 700 students sign petition', *Wales Online*, 5 November 2014, walesonline.co.uk/whats-on/comedy-news/cardiff-university-students-union-cancels-8052634.
16. 'Anti-Lad Culture Policy', Cardiff University Students' Union, 3 December 2013, cardiffstudents.com/pageassets/about-cusu/policy/Anti-Lad-Culture-Policy.pdf.
17. *That's What She Said: Women Students' Experiences of 'Lad Culture' in Higher Education*, by Alison Phipps and Isabel Young, National Union of Students, 8 March 2013, nus.org.uk/en/nus-calls-for-summit-on-lad-culture/.
18. *That's What She Said*, p. 25, nus.org.uk/en/nus-calls-for-summit-on-lad-culture/.
19. *That's What She Said*, p. 39, nus.org.uk/en/nus-calls-for-summit-on-lad-culture/.
20. 'Move the "Sleepwalker" Inside the Davis Museum', Change.org, 5 February 2014, change.org/p/president-h-kim-bottomly-move-the-sleepwalker-inside-the-davis-museum.

21. 'Wellesley College president: "Sleepwalker" will stay where it is through the spring', Boston.com, 20 February 2014, boston.com/yourcampus/ news/wellesley/2014/02/wellesley_college_president_sleepwalker_will_stay_ where_it_is_through_the_spring.html.
22. 'Trigger Happy', by Jennie Jarvie, *New Republic*, 3 March 2014, newrepublic.com/ article/116842/trigger-warnings-have-spread-blogs-college-classes-thats-bad.
23. 'The Trouble With Teaching Rape Law', by Jeannie Suk, *New Yorker*, 15 December 2014, newyorker.com/news/news-desk/trouble-teaching-rape-law.
24. 'Julie Bindel vs "the stupid little bellends"', by Tim Black, *spiked*, 6 February 2015, spiked-online.com/newsite/article/julie-bindel-vs-the-stupid-little- bellends/16673#.VgkC48tViko.
25. *Only Words*, by Catharine MacKinnon, Harvard University Press, 1993, p. 107.
26. Quoted in: 'Public Opinion Turns Against Feminism', *Issues and Controversies*, 25 May 2001.
27. 'The weaker sex', *The Economist*, 7 March 2015, economist.com/news/ international/21645759-boys-are-being-outclassed-girls-both-school-and- university-and-gap.
28. 'Young women are now earning more than men – that's not sexist, just fair', by Gaby Hinsliff, *Guardian*, 27 November 2011, theguardian.com/ commentisfree/2011/nov/27/young-women-earning-more-men.
29. 'In US, a decline in domestic violence', by Stacy Teicher Khadaroo, *Christian Science Monitor*, 26 August 2014, csmonitor.com/World/ Progress-Watch/2014/0826/In-US-a-decline-in-domestic-violence.
30. 'Murder rate drops, but mind your bags and padlock the garden shed', by Richard Ford, *The Times*, 19 July 2012, thetimes.co.uk/tto/news/uk/crime/ article3480607.ece.
31. *The End of Men*, by Hanna Rosin, Riverhead Books, 2012, pp. 176–177.
32. 'Explaining the Gender Wage Gap', by Sarah Jane Glynn, Center for American Progress, 19 May 2014, americanprogress.org/issues/economy/ report/2014/05/19/90039/explaining-the-gender-wage-gap/.
33. 'Modern Parenthood', by Kim Parker and Wendy Wang, Pew Research Center, 14 March 2013, pewsocialtrends.org/2013/03/14/modern-parent- hood-roles-of-moms-and-dads-converge-as-they-balance-work-and-family/.
34. 'Rise of the modern FeMEnist – Latest Netmums Survey Results', *Netmums*, 17 October 2012, netmums.com/coffeehouse/general-coffeehouse-chat-514/ news-current-affairs-topical-discussion-12/836486-rise-modern-femenist- latest-netmums-survey-results-all.html.
35. 'Only 18 percent of Americans consider themselves feminists', by Sarah Kliff, *Vox*, 6 April 2015, vox.com/2015/4/8/8372417/feminist-gender-equality-poll.
36. 'Feminism and the Turn Against Enlightenment', by Brendan O'Neill, *spiked*, 11 June 2015, spiked-online.com/newsite/article/feminism-and-the-turn- against-enlightenment/17057#.VgkQYMtViko.

3
Re-Educating Men: The War on Lads and Frats

Tom Slater

They say there no more rebels. Spend half an hour on a modern university campus and you start to wonder why.

Where once students went to university to get away from small-town stuffiness and the parental yoke, students today arrive on campus to find an even more stifling climate than the one they left behind. Campus life is sanitised – cleansed of offensive words, 'triggering' ideas and, increasingly, booze. In 2014, the UK National Union of Students (NUS) signed up to a government anti-binge-drinking initiative, undermining any claim it might have had to representing the interests of its members.[1]

In such an uptight atmosphere, it's easier than ever to rebel, to say or do something out-of-line. And yet, with few noble exceptions, very few do. Today, with so many students willing to toe the moral line, the job of riling the campus thought police has fallen solely to those students who are offensive as a matter of course. They are the sort of young men who go out on a night out dressed up as Osama bin Laden and would rather be thrown out of a bar for vomiting up a wall than back out of a drinking contest. In the UK, we call them lads, a macho subset of the student population who delight in sport, lager, mock-sexist 'banter' and chasing women. In the US, it's frat boys, those hard-partying, panty-raiding fiends who line the houses on Greek Row.

Both lad and frat culture developed out of a desire on the part of male undergraduates to rebel against stifling standards of behaviour. Fraternities began in the US in the 1820s as small, masonic-inspired societies, set up by male students so they could organise, and party, free of their overbearing minders. Lad culture, by contrast, is a much more recent phenomenon. It began in the 1990s in reaction to a new, politically correct standard of masculinity called 'the new man',[2] with swathes of young British men adopting a kind of caricature of working-class culture. Today, fraternities span over 800 colleges and are represented by moneyed national executives, but they remain at the centre of university social life. And while British lad culture is a more amorphous, social phenomenon, its presence is very much felt on campus today through university sports teams and their notoriously raucous 'socials'.

Unsurprisingly, in the intolerant climate of the modern university, lads and frats have been getting into a lot of trouble of late. They've been suspended, banned, expelled and, in some cases, re-educated. They've been smeared as sexists, racists and even latent sex offenders, and become the subject of national campaigns to clean up their act. It's among the most vicious crusades campuses have seen in decades. And within it, you get a glimpse of just how conformist campus culture has become.

LSE

On 7 October 2014, the men's rugby team at the London School of Economics (LSE) was disbanded after it distributed leaflets at the university freshers' fair that contained 'offensive and stigmatising language'.[3] The literature in question warned new students about picking up STDs from 'sloppy birds', jibed that 'homosexual debauchery' was forbidden for all team members and referred to the women's team as 'beast-like'. In short, it was a bad joke – a grossly offensive send-up of the anodyne welcome literature that university societies distribute each year at freshers' fairs across the UK. But LSE's students' union (LSESU) wasn't laughing.

After no one in the team claimed responsibility, LSESU president Nona Buckley-Irvine announced that the entire team would be banned for the rest of the academic year. 'Our actions in disbanding the club demonstrate the seriousness of the situation, and our commitment to challenging cultures that allow misogyny, sexism and homophobia to exist', she said in a statement.[4] And the punishment didn't stop there. Taking Buckley-Irvine's lead, a few of the rugby players formed a working group that pledged to reform the culture within the team. Over the course of the academic year, they performed various acts of public contrition in order to earn back their privileges, including standing outside LSE buildings holding pro-feminist placards[5] and agreeing to play a charity match against a local gay men's team.[6]

It was a startling spectacle. An entire student society was shut down overnight – and submitted to public shaming – because of the actions of a few of its members. All for the heinous crime of making bad jokes. But as shocking as the LSE Men's Rugby ban was, it is but one in a long line of similar scandals across the UK and US. Just over a month after LSE Men's Rugby hung up their boots, another group of young men across the Atlantic suffered an even more illiberal fate.

UVA

On 19 November 2014, an article was published in *Rolling Stone* that would send a shockwave through the US college establishment. 'A Rape on Campus: A Brutal Assault and Struggle for Justice at UVA', written by *Rolling Stone* staffer Sabrina Rubin Erdely, told a stark story about a gang rape that was alleged to have occurred in the Phi Kappa Psi fraternity house at the University of Virginia (UVA) in 2012.[7] The article's subject, a student referred to as 'Jackie', claimed she had been attacked by seven Phi Kappa Psi members as part of a horrific, premeditated initiation ceremony. The details were sadistic and grim. She claimed she had been thrown through a glass table, referred to as 'it' and raped for three hours. After her ordeal, Jackie said her friends, finding her shaken and her dress covered in blood, told her not to go to the authorities.

After the article was published, UVA student activists picketed the Phi Kappa Psi fraternity house, threw bottles and cinderblocks through its windows and sprayed its outer walls in graffiti – one tag dubbing it the 'UVA Center for RAPE'.[8] UVA's president, Teresa Sullivan, was called on to take immediate action. After prevaricating for a few days, Sullivan announced on 25 November that, in response to the revelations, *all* UVA fraternities would be suspended until January while the university and the police conducted their respective investigations.[9]

Sullivan was praised for taking decisive action, but, as the days and weeks drew on, the *Rolling Stone* story began to unravel. An investigation by the *Washington Post* revealed that one of the young men Jackie named as one of her attackers didn't belong to Phi Kappa Psi; no member of the fraternity worked as a lifeguard, as she claimed one of her attackers did; her friends claimed that when they met her after the party she showed no signs of injury; and one particular friend, who connected with Jackie over her alleged ordeal, said that she had originally claimed she was attacked by five men, before changing the number to seven.[10]

Rolling Stone recanted,[11] but the crusade was already underway. Some commentators maintained they still 'believed' Jackie's story[12]; others insisted that, even if these allegations were now in doubt, discounting them altogether would 'send the wrong message' to rape survivors. Under such intense moral pressure, Sullivan maintained the ban on fraternities, establishing an 'Ad Hoc Group on University Climate and Culture', which would seek to address 'a long history of problems [in UVA fraternity life] around power and privilege involving gender and race'.[13] The ban was lifted in January 2015 on the condition that fraternities sign agreements entailing certain restrictions on parties taking place after 9pm.[14] As the new semester began, and fraternities hesitantly signed up to the new deal, Charlottesville Police Department announced their investigation had found no 'substantive basis to confirm that the allegations raised in the *Rolling Stone* article occurred'.[15]

A 'pack' mentality

While LSE and UVA seem like two very different cases, the response of the institutions involved was strikingly similar. Minor or, in the UVA frat's case, *alleged* misconduct was used as a pretext to clamp down on the free association of an entire group of young men. Rather than isolate and deal with individual wrongdoing, both UVA and LSESU decided to enact humiliating collective punishment. And these weren't isolated examples, either. On both sides of the Atlantic, university campuses are in the grip of a full-blown moral panic about the behaviour of rowdy young men.

Feminist campaigners and students' unions in the UK have attempted a cultural cleansing of laddishness from campuses: SUs at Aberdeen, Bournemouth, Derby, Lancaster and Swansea have banned soft-porn 'lads' mags' from campus shops; Brunel, Chester, Huddersfield, Newcastle and Reading have banned sports-team initiation ceremonies; and, in November 2014, Cardiff University Students' Union banned Dapper Laughs (the parodic, lad alter-ego of comedian Daniel O'Reilly) from performing at a union venue – helping to kickstart a national campaign to have his TV show cancelled.[16]

In the US, the campaign against frats has been no less unhinged – marked by brutal overreactions to offensive speech and minor indiscretions. In March 2015, the Sigma Alpha Epsilon chapter at the University of Oklahoma (OU) was disbanded indefinitely when a video of its members singing a racist chant appeared online.[17] As vile as their behaviour was, the chant was First Amendment-protected speech, which OU, as a publicly funded body, had no legal right to curtail. Nevertheless, it was what happened next that was most revealing. After the OU story broke, it was open season on frats across the US – and it wasn't just racist speech that marked them out for censure. That same month, North Carolina

State University disbanded its chapter of Pi Kappa Phi when a notebook containing rape jokes was found at an off-campus restaurant.[18] The Washburn University chapter of Phi Delta Pheta was disbanded when it was revealed they had made sexist jokes, such as 'Remember, women are objects', in *private* text messages.[19] And, later that year, fraternities at Old Dominion University[20] and Middle Tennessee State University[21] were suspended for hanging signs on their houses during welcome week, bearing such slogans as 'Freshman girl info center' and 'Go ahead and drop mom off too …'. While some of these frats were disbanded by their own national executives, the moral pressure from student campaigners and campus bureaucrats to punish frats for such minor indiscretions was intense.

Underlying this crusade is a sense that these young men are easily led – both by the culture they consume and the other men they surround themselves with. The NUS has smeared lad culture as a 'pack mentality' that is 'sexist, misogynist and homophobic'.[22] And, according to a writer for *Time*, 'frats breed sexism and misogyny that lasts long after college'.[23] The problem, they claim, is not their minor indiscretions, but the darker attitudes they expose. The moral distinction between words and actions, between enjoying sexist humour and being a dangerous misogynist, is deemed irrelevant. Individual responsibility is supposedly consumed by the will of the 'pack'. And this sentiment has led to calls to stamp out lad and frat culture altogether. In January 2014, *Bloomberg* published an editorial making the case for *all* universities to abolish fraternities.[24] In the UK, the NUS has held a summit, formed a national strategy team and started a pilot scheme at nine universities with the stated aim of 'confronting' lad culture.[25]

There's no doubting that lads and frats can be deeply offensive – and, as the rest of this book will attest, students can get in trouble for saying and doing much less on a modern university campus. But the sheer scale of the backlash has been unprecedented. Lads and frats have always caused headaches for campus administrators – and irritated students who go to university to learn more than how to down a dirty pint. But, in the past, this behaviour was generally tolerated. It was recognised that young men at university, many of them away from home for the first time, often act up, rebel and carry on in a way that they wouldn't in everyday life. They are prone to push the boundaries of acceptable speech in a way that is juvenile, but otherwise harmless. The harsh response from universities and students' unions of late reveals a clear shift. Today, lads and frats are being treated not only as offensive, but as morally deficient; their crudity is deemed indicative of dark propensities that must be reined in. In the following section, we'll explore why.

'One in five'

In 2007, a government-funded study into the rate of sexual violence on campus was published. Commissioned by the US Department of Justice, and based on an online survey of 6,841 students, the *Campus Sexual Assault (CSA) Study* found that 19 per cent (roughly one in five) female respondents said they had been the victim of 'attempted or completed sexual assault' during their time at college.[26] This headline figure was held up by the press and campus campaigners as proof that there was an epidemic of rape and sexual assault on university campuses. There was a 'rape culture', many claimed, in which sexual assault was not only rife, but actively encouraged.

'One in five' became a rallying cry, and the existence of rape culture an article of faith. Sabrina Rubin Erdely said she set out to write the UVA *Rolling Stone* piece because she wanted to tackle 'this pervasive culture of sexual harassment/rape culture' on campus.[27] And it caught the attention of student politicos in the UK, too. In 2010, the NUS published its own sexual-assault study called *Hidden Marks*. Comprising a national online survey of 2,058 participants, it claimed that one in seven women had experienced a 'serious physical or sexual assault during their time as a student'.[28] The study made national headlines and led students' unions across the country to adopt stringent sexual-harassment policies.

These two studies have proved so influential that even the US and UK governments have taken notice. The US Office for Civil Rights and US Department of Education have handed down edicts, in 2011[29] and 2013[30] respectively, to lower the standard of proof in campus sexual-assault hearings and broaden the definition of sexual harassment. And, in September 2015, UK business secretary Sajid Javid called on British universities to set up a taskforce to tackle the issue of sexual assault and harassment on campuses.[31] But in all of the official clamour to Do Something about this new epidemic of sexual violence, something crucial was missed: neither the *Campus Sexual Assault Study* nor *Hidden Marks* were worth the paper they were printed on.

From the outset, there were clearly limitations to the *CSA* study; its sample was small and unrepresentative, making it difficult for the findings to be generalised. But, as sceptics began to dig into the data, they found that, even then, 'one in five' was deeply misleading. The researchers conflated a vast range of experiences, from unwanted kissing and fondling to forced penetration and rape. What's more, as journalist Cathy Young has pointed out, 70 per cent of the incidents reported were marked as 'drug- and/or or alcohol-enabled', despite the fact that 'two-thirds of the college women whom the study counted as victims of drug- or alcohol-enabled rape did not think they were raped'.[32] The researchers, it seemed, were redefining their participants' drunken sexual experiences as non-consensual.

When researchers compared *CSA* to other studies, they found huge discrepancies. As academic and author Christina Hoff Sommers pointed out, statistics compiled by the Bureau of Justice put the rate of rape and sexual assault at closer to one in 40. 'One in 40 is still too many women', she wrote. 'But it hardly constitutes a "rape culture" requiring White House intervention.'[33] After a while, the *CSA* study was so roundly criticised that even its authors wrote an article for *Time* urging people to take 'one in five' with a pinch of salt: 'There are caveats that make it inappropriate to use the one-in-five number.'[34]

Hidden Marks didn't stand up to much scrutiny, either. Like the *CSA* study, its sample was small, its participants were self-selecting, and its definitions were shockingly broad. The 'one in seven' stat comprised a wide range of experiences, from 'touching over clothes' to 'unwanted kissing' to general *physical* assault. And, once again, there seemed to be a disjoint between how the participants and the researchers interpreted certain incidents, as 65 per cent of the women that made up the 'one in seven' stat 'didn't think [their experience] was serious enough to report'.[35] For some, this was a damning indictment – victims, they thought, were scared of coming forward. In truth, it seemed that most respondents recognised that awkward or ungentlemanly come-ons are not the same as sexual assault.

This transatlantic panic about campus rape culture has fuelled the war on lads and frats. The heavy-handed treatment of UVA fraternities, the willingness of the administration to accept unsubstantiated claims at face value, was a direct result of the hysteria generated by these dodgy stats. Similarly, while the banning of LSE Men's Rugby may have appeared a gross overreaction, in a climate in which women are said to be at constant threat of sexual harassment, and young men are, according to the NUS, blinded by the 'rape-supportive attitudes'[36] encased in laddish culture, it begins to look like a prudent move.

These sorts of claims were made despite the fact that, putting aside their manifest flaws, neither the *CSA* study nor *Hidden Marks* made any link between sexual assault and lad or frat culture – while others have tried, and failed, to connect the dots. In 2013, academic John Foubert claimed his own research proved that 'fraternity men are three times more likely to rape'[37] – in fact, the 2007 study merely claimed that fraternity men were three times more likely to procure sex by means of a 'sexually coercive act', examples of which included 'telling lies about the future'.[38] Similarly, the NUS's follow-up report, *That's What She Said*, claimed that lad culture 'could easily lead to sexual harassment'[39] – this was based on little more than musings gleaned from focus groups with self-selecting participants. As has become the norm in the war on lads and frats, prejudice is presented as fact.

I Heart Consent

Today, no campus ban is complete without an appeal to 'the statistics' and the culture of rape that lad and frat culture allegedly cultivate. The long-discredited idea that exposure to blue culture – be it nudey mags or sexist jokes – can stir dangerous impulses in young men has been completely rehabilitated and dolled up in sub-sociological terms; 'lad-culture promoters', says an Edinburgh University Students Association policy, 'trivialise rape and by doing so contribute to a culturally permissible attitude to rape'.[40] In this and so many more examples young men are assigned a lower form of autonomy, and intervention is mandated in an attempt to quell the impulses and influences they are unaware are affecting them. It is this lowly view that has led campus politicos to take one chilling step further. Rather than simply try to cover students' eyes and ears from the influences that may corrupt them, they have decided to cut out the middleman, get inside students' heads and correct their dodgy ideas before they get a chance to act on them. The panic has paved the way for re-education and the regulation of students' sex lives.

This trend is most starkly seen in the development of interventions and workshops aimed at pre-empting sexual harassment, sexual assault and rape – particularly in the UK. In 2014, the NUS launched its 'I Heart Consent' campaign. As part of a pilot scheme of 20 universities, it set up consent workshops aimed at 'rectifying problematic perspectives of consent' and advocating that students procure 'enthusiastic consent' before engaging in any sexual act.[41] The issues raised by this new standard of sexual consent – commonly referred to as 'affirmative consent' in the US – are too vast to explore in much detail here. As US author and lawyer Wendy Kaminer has pointed out, affirmative consent is, at the very least, 'difficult to reconcile with the realities of sexual interactions', in which consent is often implicit.[42] But, in any case, the swiftness

with which these new and controversial programmes were imposed on
students was revealing.

While some UK universities have made consent workshops compul-
sory for all first-years, they have been disproportionately pushed on
sports teams. In May 2015, the University of Oxford made consent
training a requirement for all college rugby teams to compete in inter-
college tournaments.[43] After the University of Sussex's men's rugby
team caused £15,000 worth of damage to their tour bus in 2013, the
team captains were required to train as I Heart Consent facilitators and
hold workshops throughout the year.[44] While no one would deny the
team should have been punished, the choice of punishment here was
startling – as if their wanton act of destruction was a harbinger of worse
atrocities to come.

Of all the aspects of the campus war on young men, consent classes
have generated the most kickback from students. George Lawlor, a student at the University of Warwick, became a viral hit when he wrote
an article for the *Tab* rejecting being 'taught not to be a rapist'.[45] A few,
days later, Jack Hadfield, another Warwick student, penned a piece for
Breitbart, claiming that 'this new obsession with affirmative, ongoing
consent, perpetuated by wacky third-wave feminists' is 'demonising'
young men.[46] But, as welcome as it was, this kickback failed to grasp
what is really going on. This is not a feminist war on men. After all,
this crusade depends as much on a notion of imperilled, vulnerable and
thin-skinned young women, as it does a volatile notion of young men.

What the war on lads and frats reveals is a far deeper interventionist
dynamic that paints all students as either in need of protection or control. Consent classes are the natural progression of the project of campus
censorship itself. Once you concede that students are too vulnerable to
navigate the world of ideas unsupervised, it is only logical that this remit
will be extended to their social and sexual lives. And, as we will see, this
is something campus freedom-fighters have always recognised.

In loco parentis

The original demand for free speech on campus went hand in hand
with the insistence that students were adults, capable of negotiating
the social and sexual, as well as intellectual, sphere for themselves.
When students in the 1960s were rebelling against the censorious,
Red-scare climate on university campuses – pioneered by the Free
Speech Movement in Berkeley in 1964 – their core demand was an
end to the *in loco parentis* responsibilities universities held over them.

In loco parentis was used to justify restrictions on speech and political activity, but it also mandated curfews and the regulation of students', and particular female students', sex lives. As dissident feminist Camille Paglia reflected recently, 'When I arrived in college in 1964 *in loco parentis* was operative. I was in a girl's dorm, we had to sign in at 11 o'clock at night, while the boys could run free ... My generation of women rose up and said [to the university] get out of our private lives!'[47] That the transatlantic fight for free speech on campus coincided with the call for an end to the regulation of students' private lives was no coincidence.

Today, the explosion of campus censorship has rehabilitated the regulation of students' sex lives, formalising it in consent workshops in the UK and, more chillingly, new state laws in New York and California mandating that students attain 'affirmative consent' before engaging in any sexual act.[48] That it is students themselves – or, at least, their own representative bodies – who are advocating for these creepy regimes speaks to the parlous state campus freedom is in. Not only are students insisting they be protected from words, but also from one another. This is the complete inversion of the 60s student project; students today want universities to play parent. What's more, even anti-censorship students have so far failed to grasp quite how illiberal the consent-class phenomenon is, and how intertwined it is with campus censorship itself. Indeed, while various censorship scandals in the UK have provoked outrage from principled students, the rise of consent classes has sparked nowhere near as much outrage – aside from Lawlor and Hadfield, few students have stuck their heads above the parapet.

Against the creeping return of *in loco parentis*, lads and frats are both the primary targets and the last line of defence. Whether it was the early frat boys rebelling against the puritanical regimes of 19th-century colleges, or 90s lads kicking back against suffocating political correctness, they have always resisted any threat to their fun. They become crasser, more offensive, more wilfully provocative, as the fetters begin to be felt. Today, that rebellious muscle continues to twitch. As one writer remarked, the closest thing to a 60s rebel you'll find on campus today is 'the moron over at Phi Sigma Kappa who plans the Colonial Bros and Nava-Hos mixer'.[49]

It's not big and it's not clever, but in an age of such stifling conformity, the rebelliousness of lads and frats should be cherished.

Tom Slater *is deputy editor at* spiked *and coordinator of the Free Speech University Rankings.*

Notes

1. 'University campaign to counter binge-drinking culture', BBC News, 28 May 2014, bbc.com/news/education-27589939.
2. 'It is Happening for a Reason: An Interview with Pamela Church Gibson', by Agnieszka Graff, *Americanist*, Vol 24, p. 28, asc.uw.edu.pl/theamericanist/vol/24/24_15-32.pdf.
3. '"Sexist" rugby team banned over leaflet "mocking women"', BBC, 7 October 2014, bbc.co.uk/newsbeat/article/29530810/sexist-rugby-team-banned-over-leaflet-mocking-women.
4. 'Updated statement about the LSE Men's Rugby Club', LSE Students' Union, lsesu.tumblr.com/post/99409601163/updated-statement-about-the-lse-mens-rugby-club.
5. 'Say goodbye to the "bad" lads', *Tab*, 10 February 2015, thetab.com/uk/lse/2015/02/10/say-goodbye-to-the-bad-lads-1126.
6. 'Tackling Sexism and Homophobia in Rugby', LSE, llse.ac.uk/publicEvents/events/2015/11/20151110t1830vSSH.aspx.
7. 'A Rape on Campus: A Brutal Assault and Struggle for Justice at UVA', by Sabrina Rubin Erdely, *Rolling Stone*, 19 November 2014, *since retracted*.
8. 'UVA Fraternity House Vandalized', NBC 29, 20 November 2014, nbc29.com/story/27439468/uva-fraternity-house-vandalized.
9. 'UVA suspends fraternities after report on gang rape allegation', CNN, 25 November 2014, edition.cnn.com/2014/11/22/us/university-of-virginia-sexual-assault-allegations/.
10. 'Key elements of Rolling Stone's U-Va. gang rape allegations in doubt', *Washington Post*, 5 December 2014, washingtonpost.com/local/education/u-va-fraternity-to-rebut-claims-of-gang-rape-in-rolling-stone/2014/12/05/5fa5f7d2-7c91-11e4-84d4-7c896b90abdc_story.html.
11. 'A Note to Our Readers', *Rolling Stone*, 5 December 2014, rollingstone.com/culture/news/a-note-to-our-readers-20141205.
12. 'Who is Jackie? Rolling Stone's rape story is about a person – and I believe her', by Jessica Valenti, *Guardian*, 8 December 2014, theguardian.com/commentisfree/2014/dec/08/who-is-jackie-rolling-stone-rape-story.
13. 'Ad hoc committee addresses University culture, Greek life, sexual assault', *Cavalier Daily*, 8 December 2014, cavalierdaily.com/article/2014/12/president-creates-ad-hoc-committee.
14. 'Post-Scandal, UVA Frat Parties Rage On', *Bloomberg*, 21 January 2015, bloomberg.com/news/articles/2015-01-21/post-scandal-uva-frat-parties-rage-on.
15. 'UVA Reinstates Phi Kappa Psi After Gang Rape Investigation', *Bloomberg*, 12 January 2015, bloomberg.com/news/articles/2015-01-12/uva-reinstates-phi-kappa-psi-frat-after-gang-rape-investigation.
16. Free Speech University Rankings, *spiked*, spiked-online.com/free-speech-university-rankings.
17. 'University Oklahoma Fraternity Caught Singing Awful Racist Chant (FULL VIDEO)', YouTube, 9 March 2015, youtube.com/watch?v=RdtfKYitMDI.
18. 'Fraternity at NC disbanded after sickening lynching and rape entries are found in pledge book', *Daily Mail*, 26 March 2015, dailymail.co.uk/news/article-3012287/That-tree-perfect-lynching-NC-fraternity-DISBANDED-offensive-pledge-book-containing-lynching-rape-jokes.html.

19. 'Washburn University Phi Delta Theta Suspended During Investigation Into Fraternity Brothers' "Inappropriate" Text Messages', *International Business Times*, 16 April 2015, ibtimes.com/washburn-university-phi-delta-theta-suspended-during-investigation-fraternity-1885124.
20. 'A Common Sign', *Inside Higher Ed*, 28 August 2015, insidehighered.com/news/2015/08/28/sexist-banners-old-dominion-point-practice-many-campuses.
21. 'MTSU frat suspended pending investigation after sign reads "FRESHMAN GIRLS INFO CENTER"', WKRN, 25 August 2015, wkrn.com/2015/08/25/mtsu-fraternity-removes-freshman-girls-info-center-banner-from-house/.
22. *That's What She Said: Women Students' Experiences of 'Lad Culture' in Higher Education*, by Alison Phipps and Isabel Young, National Union of Students, 2013, p. 32, nus.org.uk/Global/Campaigns/That's%20what%20she%20said%20full%20report%20Final%20web.pdf.
23. 'The Problem With Frats Isn't Just Rape. It's Power', by Jessica Bennett, *Time*, 3 December 2014, time.com/3616158/fraternity-rape-uva-rolling-stone-sexual-assault/.
24. 'Dean Wormer's Favorite Editorial', Bloomberg, 7 January 2014, bloomberg-view.com/articles/2014-01-07/dean-wormer-s-favorite-editorial.
25. 'Lad Culture', NUS Connect, nusconnect.org.uk/winning-for-students/women/lad-culture.
26. *The Campus Sexual Assault (CSA) Study*, by Christopher P Krebs et al, US Department of Justice, December 2007, p. xviii, ncjrs.gov/pdffiles1/nij/grants/221153.pdf.
27. 'Rolling Stone and UVA: The Columbia University Graduate School of Journalism Report', *Rolling Stone*, 5 April 2015, rollingstone.com/culture/features/a-rape-on-campus-what-went-wrong-20150405.
28. *Hidden Marks: A Study of Women Students' Experiences of Harassment, Stalking, Violence and Sexual Assault*, National Union of Students, March 2010, p. 3, nus.org.uk/en/news/1-in-7-women-students-is-a-victim-of-sexual-assault-or-violence1/.
29. 'Dear Colleague', US Department of Education, 4 April 2011, www2.ed.gov/about/offices/list/ocr/letters/colleague-201104.pdf.
30. 'Dear Colleague Letter', US Department of Education, 24 April 2013, www2.ed.gov/about/offices/list/ocr/letters/colleague-201304.html.
31. 'Government orders inquiry over violence against women at universities', *Guardian*, 6 September 2015, theguardian.com/education/2015/sep/06/government-inquiry-violence-against-women-at-universities.
32. 'Guilty Until Proven Innocent: The Skewed White House Crusade on Sexual Assault', by Cathy Young, *Time*, 6 May 2014, time.com/88407/the-white-houses-report-on-campus-sexual-assault-relies-on-the-lowest-common-denominator/.
33. 'Rape Culture Is a "Panic Where Paranoia, Censorship, and False Accusations Flourish"', by Christina Hoff Sommers, *Time*, 15 May 2014, time.com/100091/campus-sexual-assault-christina-hoff-sommers/.
34. 'Setting the Record Straight on "1 in 5"', *Time*, 15 December 2014, time.com/3633903/campus-rape-1-in-5-sexual-assault-setting-record-straight/.
35. *Hidden Marks*, p. 21, nus.org.uk/en/news/1-in-7-women-students-is-a-victim-of-sexual-assault-or-violence1/.

36. *That's What She Said*, p. 28 nus.org.uk/Global/Campaigns/That's%20 what%20she%20said%20full%20report%20Final%20web.pdf.
37. '"Rapebait" email reveals dark side of frat culture', by John Foubert, CNN, 9 October 2013, edition.cnn.com/2013/10/09/opinion/foubert-fraternities-rape/.
38. 'Behavior Differences Seven Months Later: Effects of a Rape Prevention Program', by John D Foubert et al, *NASPA Journal*, Vol 44, No 4, 2007, researchgate.net/profile/John_Foubert/publication/230687915_Behavior_Differences_Seven_Months_Later_Effects_of_a_Rape_Prevention_Program/links/0fcfd502fbec2a7aef000000.pdf.
39. *That's What She Said*, p. 37 nus.org.uk/Global/Campaigns/That's%20 what%20she%20said%20full%20report%20Final%20web.pdf.
40. 'End Rape Culture and Lad Banter on Campus', EUSA, 11 March 2013, eusa. ed.ac.uk/eusapolicy/liberation/endrapeculture/.
41. 'I Heart Consent: Consent Workshop Facilitator Guide', National Union of Students, 2014, nusconnect.org.uk/resources/i-heart-consent-guide.
42. 'Don't expect students to follow new sexual consent rules', by Wendy Kaminer, *Boston Globe*, 27 July 2015, bostonglobe.com/opinion/2015/07/26/ don-expect-students-follow-new-sexual-consent-rules/D2ui6BG7WxUszVpgpv ABmM/story.html.
43. 'Oxford University sends rugby players to anti-sexism classes', *Telegraph*, 9 May 2015, telegraph.co.uk/news/uknews/11594642/Oxford-University-sends-rugby-players-to-anti-sexism-classes.html.
44. 'Sussex's rugby boys react to LSE ban', *Tab*, 12 October 2014, thetab.com/uk/ sussex/2014/10/12/sussexs-rugby-boys-react-to-lse-ban-4257.
45. 'Why I don't need consent lessons', by George Lawlor, *Tab*, 14 October 2015, thetab.com/uk/warwick/2015/10/14/dont-need-consent-lessons-9925.
46. 'I'm a student, and I too decline to attend "consent classes"', by Jack Hadfield, *Breitbart*, 16 October 2015, breitbart.com/big-government/2015/10/16/im-a-student-and-i-too-decline-to-attend-consent-classes/.
47. 'Everything's Awesome and Camille Paglia is Unhappy!', YouTube, 19 March 2015, youtube.com/watch?v=88_3AhU0-B0.
48. 'Affirmative Consent: Are Students Really Asking?', by Sandy Keenan, *New York Times*, 28 July 2015, nytimes.com/2015/08/02/education/edlife/affirmative-consent-are-students-really-asking.html?_r=0.
49. 'That's Not Funny!', by Caitlin Flanagan, *Atlantic*, September 2015, theatlantic. com/magazine/archive/2015/09/thats-not-funny/399335/.

4

Teaching Students to Censor: How Academics Betrayed Free Speech

Joanna Williams

Today, the most insidious threats to free speech on campus do not come from legislating governments or controlling institutional managers. That some students are at the forefront of calling for debates to be cancelled, songs banned and course content to come with trigger warnings has been well documented. It would be easy to get the impression that while students seek freedom *from* speech and desire to turn the university into an emotional and intellectual Safe Space, academics look on in horror and champion the cause of free speech. Often, however, such students are simply putting into practice the ideas of their lecturers. Academics have taught and legitimised the notion that words and images harm, that people should be protected from offence and that restricting free speech is the best way to achieve this aim.

There has never been a golden age when universities permitted unfettered free speech on campus. Throughout the latter half of the 19th and the first half of the 20th century, students quietly challenged the paternalistic regulations placed upon them. For the most part, their protests fell on deaf ears and faculty continued to consider students as intellectually innocent, easily corruptible and in need of firm discipline. It was not until the 1960s that students' demands for free speech began to be taken seriously and, in Europe and America, they successfully challenged the institutional restrictions on their liberty. In the UK, universities lifted *in loco parentis* legislation in 1970, when the legal age of majority was lowered from 21 to 18. Yet, even at that very moment, new arguments against free speech were being marshalled. However, this time they did not come from university authorities, but from politically radical lecturers influenced by academic trends such as critical theory, postmodernism and feminism.

Nowadays it can often seem as if academics are as likely to be involved in calls to restrict free speech as they are to defend academic freedom. In the summer of 2015, Nobel Prize-winning biochemist Sir Tim Hunt was publicly criticised by fellow scientists and academics following a self-deprecating joke he made about the 'problem' of women in laboratories. That he is married to leading immunologist Mary Collins and has a track record of supporting and advancing women's careers in science did not prevent a public outcry over the supposedly damaging impact of his unguarded comment. When Hunt's resignation from his honorary position at University College London (UCL) was accepted, rather than defending his right to free speech, a number of prominent academics expressed satisfaction that he had demonstrably been punished for his crime of having uttered a sexist remark. Through incidents such as this, students learn that language is considered a cause of oppression and that those speaking out of turn will be publicly humiliated.

Rather than teaching critical thinking, universities all too often induct the next generation into how to conform to the expected speech and behaviour codes of right-thinking, polite society. When scholars encourage the abandonment of truth, question the possibility of knowledge and seek to restrict free speech, it should come as little surprise to see students endorse this mission. This chapter considers the intellectual developments that have occurred in the academy over the past few decades and have given rise to a climate that finds free speech so threatening.

Critical theory

For several decades, the influence of critical theory and post-structuralism has been all-pervasive within university humanities departments throughout Europe and North America. Critical theory developed from the work of the Frankfurt School, a group of philosophers who moved from Germany to America at the time of the Second World War. Scholars such as Theodor Adorno, Max Horkheimer and Herbert Marcuse sought to marry philosophy, sociology and psychology, in particular the works of Marx and Freud, to explain why the working class in Western Europe had not engaged in revolution as had their Russian contemporaries. Later, the focus shifted to explaining why the majority of German citizens went along with the descent into barbarism marked by the rise of fascism, while Russia's Communist revolution had given way to Stalin's totalitarianism. They argued that the seductive power of images and language, through creating false needs and selling a consumer lifestyle, had become fundamental to the continuation of capitalism.

This foregrounding of images and vocabulary paved the way for an understanding of words as all-powerful in shaping not just a dominant ideology, but perceptions of reality itself. One key topic of interest was the role culture played in propagating a myth of people as autonomous individuals who were able to exercise free choice. Critical theorists argued that people laboured under an illusion of personal freedom and had been hoodwinked into believing that it was possible to be in control of their own destinies. It was language, which Horkheimer and Adorno argued was 'an instrument of power',[1] that helped cultivate the myth of personal freedom. Only an elite group of scholars had the insight supposedly necessary to realise that people do not have individual freedom, but simply play out an allotted role within a predetermined system.

This understanding led Marcuse to question the possibility of free expression. He argued:

> Freedom of thought, speech and conscience were – just as free enterprise, which they served to promote and protect – essentially critical ideas, designed to replace an obsolescent material and intellectual culture by a more productive and rational one. Once institutionalized, these rights and liberties shared the fate of the society of which they had become an integral part. The achievement cancels the premises.[2]

Marcuse is correct to identify the significance of free speech in allowing societies to move from a 'know your place' feudalism to capitalism premised upon a notion of 'economic individualism'. However, Marcuse assumes that once free-market capitalism has been established, free speech becomes incorporated within this all-encompassing system and rendered meaningless. As freedom within the system is illusory, and real freedom is only to be found outside of the system, so, too, he argues, is free speech an elaborate myth.

This view was later reinforced by structuralists, who built upon the work of the Swiss linguist Ferdinand de Saussure. Saussure highlighted the arbitrary relationship between language (signifiers) and reality (signified). Structuralists went further in suggesting that language itself shaped people's perceptions of reality. The French philosopher Michel Foucault took these arguments to their logical conclusion. He argued that language does not simply represent or shape people's perceptions of reality, but that reality is actually constructed through language. He suggested that discourse could no longer be treated as 'groups of signs (signifying elements referring to contents or representations) but as practices that systematically form the objects of which they speak'.[3] For Foucault, there is nothing other than language: 'One remains within the dimension of discourse.'[4]

Similarly, for later post-structuralists, words refer only to other signifiers without ever reaching a final signified. The French psychoanalyst Jacques Lacan's statement that 'It is the world of words that creates the world of things'[5] echoed Foucault's emphasis on discourse. The French philosopher Jacques Derrida further emphasised this point with his claim that, 'There is nothing outside of the text'.[6] Derrida denies that meaning is first embodied outside of language and then captured, or reflected in it. Instead, he asserts that meaning is an effect of, or produced through, language. Derrida suggests that as texts are all form and no content, then arriving at meaning is impossible and we only see the world through an endless interplay of differences; meaning becomes difference.

Such theorists turn an older interpretation of Marxism on its head. Rather than material and economic circumstances shaping reality, they argue reality is constructed through language, images and culture. They claim that cultural change alone can bring about a new consciousness among the working class and that this, in turn, can lead to more structural changes in society. This leads to the politically driven notion that changing language could become a means of altering power relationships and bringing about social justice.

If text, or 'discourse' to use Foucault's favoured term, has no relationship to a world beyond discourse, and refers only to other text, then the unique role of the author, as the authoritative creator of the text, is called into question. According to this view, individuals are not responsible for creating a text, still less a work of literature, so much as constructing a discourse from pre-existing language and concepts. When everything, even individuals, can be considered as discourse, the aim of theory becomes the deconstruction of text and with it the deconstruction of the individual. Individuals are seen as intersubjective entities, identifiable only at the boundaries between their relationships with other individuals.

Exposing the 'myth' of individual autonomy is presented as a radical anti-capitalist critique that challenges the notion that people are willing workers and enthusiastic consumers. However it also leads to an attack not just on the possibility of individual freedom within capitalism, but on the very notion of individual autonomy and the possibility of liberty. Individuals who perceive themselves as lacking autonomy and constructed through relationships and discourse are uniquely vulnerable to attacks on their sense of self. Without control over our own destiny, aspirations for emancipation are pointless; we are reduced to the level of automatons in some unknowable and uncontrollable system. The gains of the Enlightenment, the assertion of humanity as in control of its own destiny, are surrendered.

This focus on subjectivity, constructed through discourse and in relation to other subjects, has become preeminent. Many academics working within humanities disciplines assume both a degraded notion of the individual and a greater significance of popular culture. This means that the potential impact of speech – be it in the form of an argument, song or article – is overstated, at the same time as the ability of people to engage critically with challenging or offensive speech is downplayed. When this is combined with a view that all attempts at freedom within capitalism are illusory, arguments for restricting free speech are able to gain ground. When personal identity is considered so fragile a construction and words a source of oppression, then people are encouraged to think carefully about the potentially damaging impact of any words they may utter.

Feminism

In the 1980s, the shift towards postmodernism in the academy met an emergent feminism and became embedded within academic disciplines that had already become accustomed to questioning assumptions about the nature of knowledge. Academic feminism has been most influential in shifting the direction of scholarship towards a focus on identity and a preoccupation with the vulnerable self.

The primary goal of feminist scholars has been to expose and critique knowledge that they judge to be constructed according to, or in defence of, patriarchal power relations, while enabling the construction of new knowledge that puts women, and feminism, to the fore. Some feminist academics assumed that patriarchal social relations negatively affected both men and women and prevented men from having an unbiased view of reality. More often, the slogan 'the personal is political' was enacted within the academy through the assumption that it was women's experiences within the private sphere and as subordinate members of society that gave them not just a different perspective, but a superior understanding that was grounded in a greater sensitivity to the emotional realm.

In locating claims for intellectual insight within women's experiences of subordination, feminist scholars drew a direct link between oppression and access to knowledge. It is women's status as victims of patriarchy that is assumed to give them a greater understanding than men: oppression is considered to lead women to develop a superior value system and a more finely tuned sense of morality. By this logic, the most victimised sections of society are deemed to have the best understanding of the way the world works, and academic feminism has little incentive to question the existence of either oppression or oppressors. These explicitly political aims demand that women are aware of their status as victims, yet, at the same time, celebrate this 'difference' as offering them a special intellectual and emotional understanding. It achieves this by arguing that logic and rationality are specifically masculine, and therefore negative, while subjectivity, instinct and emotion are distinctly feminine traits, and therefore positive attributes for academic work.

A politicised and feminist approach to academic work, grounded in a social constructionist assumption of gender as performative rather than biological, sat comfortably alongside a postmodernism that assumed discourse constructs not just perceptions of reality, but often reality itself. This led feminist literary theorists such as Julia Kristeva to argue that language itself creates power relations and the conditions for oppression: '[L]anguage, like culture, sets up a separation and, starting with discrete elements, concatenates an order.'[7] The American legal academic Catharine MacKinnon and the author Andrea Dworkin likewise focused on the role of language and images in propagating the oppression of women. They were particularly concerned with the alleged harm to all women that was caused by the production, distribution and consumption of pornography. The basis of their argument was that pornography was inherently discriminatory and damaging as it shaped people's thoughts about women. The US city of Indianapolis passed an ordinance (although it was later struck down) that defined pornography as discrimination. The Federal Court found the ordinance unconstitutional and described it as 'thought control'.

Other feminist scholars taught about and campaigned against sexist language, pornography and the depiction of women in the media. MacKinnon argued, 'What you need is people who see through literature like Andrea Dworkin, who see through law like me, to see through art and create the uncompromised women's visual vocabulary'.[8] The creation of such a 'visual vocabulary' led to the view that academics and students had a moral responsibility to use their feminist insight to ban images and words they perceived as oppressive. The concept of free speech was considered problematic if it allowed for the continued subjugation of oppressed groups.

Political judgements about the identity of the speaker rather than the content of what was being said were used to determine who had the right to speak. Unlike the previous era of McCarthyism, this attack on academic freedom came not from outside the university, but from within, and not from the political right, but from the radical left. From the students' perspective, censorship went from being something to rail against to a morally righteous and politically radical act. Free speech became perceived as a barrier to equality, rather than necessary for political liberation to take place. The perception that women are primarily victims, oppressed by patriarchal norms constructed through discourse, leads to the notion that debate is not to be welcomed as a means of advancing knowledge, but curtailed as an indulgent academic exercise that fails to respect people's individual truths and their own reality. These ideas, and the way they are exercised in practice, are fundamentally antithetical to free speech on campus.

Although the feminist crusade against pornography ground to a halt in the face of both new technology and the US First Amendment, the notion that words and images were pre-eminently important in shaping perceptions of reality, and could inflict mental harm upon people, remained. This view led to an increase in 'ideological policing' both inside and outside academia. There was a particular focus on the words people used. Daphne Patai and Noretta Koertge, writing in *Professing Feminism*, point out that this crusade against words, images and jokes brings modern-day feminists into line with their bourgeois Victorian fore-sisters, who saw it as their job 'to monitor language and enforce norms' of what was socially acceptable.[9] This continues today; students studying women's studies at North Carolina State University have been told they will be marked down if they use 'sexist' vocabulary such as 'mankind' in their essays. This edict was newsworthy because it was made so explicitly. But informal rules about what can and cannot be said are regularly communicated to students through example, peer-group pressure and comments from lecturers.

The inclusive university

Such trends in academic thought have been enacted in practice by university managers who, with the support of academics and students, have introduced equality and diversity policies, anti-harassment initiatives and speech codes in a bid to eliminate prejudice, regulate behaviour and create an atmosphere of respect and sensitivity. Such policies restrict free speech and censor words, images and behaviour based on a perception of offence. Rather than such policies being perceived as an infringement on free speech and students' individual rights, they are more often portrayed as necessary to protect vulnerable or 'non-traditional' students who are deemed incapable of realising intellectual autonomy and exercising rationality in relation to academic debate. It is argued that the speech of some needs to be curtailed to defend the speech rights of historically oppressed groups.

The transition that has taken place over the past two decades, from the liberal university to the 'inclusive' university, represents a fundamental shift in notions of equality, freedom and justice. The lack of any real dispute accompanying this shift illustrates the extent to which higher education had already embarked upon a wholesale rejection of liberal academic principles, creating a moral vacuum for politicised values of inclusion, equality and justice to fill. The university has gone from being an organised marketplace of ideas, responsible for the preservation and intergenerational transmission of knowledge and culture, to a community seemingly held together by a shared commitment to sensitivity and respect for one another. Victory for the inclusive university both emerges out of and further consolidates changed understandings of what it means to be a student. The concept of the student has moved from an autonomous individual, capable of mastering and contributing to a body of knowledge, to that of a vulnerable and stressed-out consumer in need of looking after.

The replacement of a clash of competing views with a focus on sensitivity and respect not only prevents free speech on campus, it often serves to enforce an intolerance of dissent. Champions of the inclusive university argue that groups assumed to have power, often on the basis of their biology, experience reality in a different way to those assumed to have less power. So, for example, white men are considered to experience the world differently to black women. This consolidates the belief that free speech needs to be limited as it is assumed that allowing people to speak freely will simply reinforce the privileges of the already powerful. Therefore, people from historically oppressed groups need special help to have their voices heard.

Some have gone so far as to suggest that the inclusive university be renamed 'the "intrusive university"' for its disruptive influence on academic freedom'.[10] The inclusive university must be challenged because 'hurt', 'emotional harm' and 'offence' are entirely subjective notions. Different people will interpret identical incidents as either offensive or simply part of the cut and thrust of university life. This lack of objectivity in defining offence contributes to a climate of self-censorship where people police their own speech and behaviour to avoid the risk that something they utter may, perhaps despite their intentions, be deemed offensive to others.

It is possible for students and lecturers to puncture the consensus created by the promotion of inclusivity and academic justice. However, a number of factors come together to make such challenges more difficult. If an academic uses the lecture theatre as pulpit or soapbox then a particular view of the topic under discussion is presented. If such a view assumes the moral high ground and appears to be shared by the majority, then it takes a very brave student indeed to challenge this consensus. The authors of the National Association of Scholars report *A Crisis of Competence* note that, 'the fixed quality of a political belief will stifle intellectual curiosity and freedom of thought when it dominates a classroom'.[11] If a student's assessed mark explicitly depends on them reproducing this political standpoint, then they would be not only brave, but potentially foolish, to question the status quo. Additionally, if students are rarely presented with knowledge that runs counter to the dominant consensus, then framing a challenge in suitably intellectual terms is difficult.

Rather than engaging in rigorous academic criticism, students are often expected to demonstrate having, through personal reflection, rejected erroneously held values in favour of a new set of officially sanctioned values. If students question such values this is only taken as proof that they have not sufficiently taken them onboard. In this way, students are socialised into the university's culture of conformity, and they run with this outside of classes and reproduce its influence beyond the campus. Students benefit from exposure to as much knowledge, and as many different values, political views and opinions, as possible. When students are taught values in the absence of knowledge, and when they are assessed on their ability to take onboard these values, rather than their ability to critique a body of knowledge, universities and academics do students a disservice.

The overt promotion of values that occurs in the inclusive university creates an orthodoxy whereby some topics are placed beyond challenge. Students are denied access to the knowledge base that is necessary in order to construct an intellectual critique of a topic. They are not presented with contestable truth claims, but with indisputable moral certainties. This can result in entire areas of research being abandoned as staff and students risk 'ostracism' if they do not fall in line with the dominant value framework. Those who disagree with the political agenda being propounded are under pressure to self-censor in order to ensure success, or to opt out and leave the academy.

Some academics are now looking on in dismay and confusion at a new generation of illiberal and censorious student activists. It is as easy, and tempting, to blame students for the collapse of free speech on campus as it is to blame government legislation or the influence of big business. But to do so would be a cowardly denial of the role that scholars themselves have played in persistently undermining the fundamental principles of academic freedom. From the first day they arrive on campus, students are taught that words and images are powerful and can hurt or corrupt; that as students they are too vulnerable, and their peers too easily led, to be exposed to potentially harmful ideas; and that the way to deal with anything that makes them feel uncomfortable is either to avoid it or, even better, to ban it.

Students should be challenged and held to account for their role in creating a climate of prurience and conformity that is anathema to debate. However, university lecturers need to be far more honest about their role in instigating, legitimising, and encouraging such restrictions. Today, the undermining of free speech happens because of scholars who, in seeking to promote academic justice over academic freedom, encourage self-censorship, close down debate and create a culture of conformity.

Joanna Williams *is education editor at* spiked *and author of* Academic Freedom in an Age of Conformity: Confronting the Fear of Knowledge.

Notes

1. *Dialectic of Enlightenment,* by Max Horkheimer and Theodor Adorno, Stanford University Press, 2002, p. 29.
2. *One-Dimensional Man*, by Herbert Marcuse, Routledge, 1991, p. 4.
3. *The Archaeology of Knowledge*, by Michel Foucault, Routledge Classics, 1989, p. 54.
4. *The Archaeology of Knowledge*, p. 85.
5. 'The Function and Field of Speech and Language in Psychoanalysis', by Jacques Lacan, In *Écrits*, WW Norton & Company, 2007, p. 229.
6. *Of Grammatology*, by Jacques Derrida, Johns Hopkins University Press, 1997.
7. *Powers of Horror*, by Julia Kristeva, Columbia University Press, 1984, p. 72
8. Quoted in: *Who Stole Feminism?*, by Christina Hoff Sommers, Simon and Schuster, 1995, p. 272.
9. *Professing Feminism, Education and Indoctrination in Women's Studies*, by Daphne Patai and Noretta Koertge, Lexington Books, 2003, p. 120.

10. 'Academic Freedom versus the Intrusive University', by John Fekete, in *Academic Freedom and the Inclusive University*, Sharon Kahn and Dennis Pavlich (eds), University of British Columbia Press, 2000, p. xv.
11. *A Crisis of Competence: The Corrupting Effect of Political Activism in the University of California*, National Association of Scholars, 2012, p. 6, nas.org/images/documents/A_Crisis_of_Competence.pdf.

5
Trigger Warnings: A Gun to the Head of Academia

Greg Lukianoff

In May 2014, the *New York Times* called attention to a new arrival on the college campus: trigger warnings.[1] Seemingly overnight, colleges and universities across America had begun fielding student demands that their professors issue content warnings before covering any material that might evoke a negative emotional response. By way of illustration, the *Times* article (titled 'Warning: The Literary Canon Could Make Students Squirm') pointed to a Rutgers student's op-ed requesting trigger warnings for *The Great Gatsby*, which apparently 'possesses a variety of scenes that reference gory, abusive and misogynistic violence', and *Mrs Dalloway*, which the student called 'a disturbing narrative' that discusses 'suicidal inclinations' and 'post-traumatic experiences'.[2] The article generated significant discussion, with readers questioning why college students would need trigger warnings – which are generally billed as a way to help those who suffer from post-traumatic stress disorder (PTSD), a serious mental-health condition – before reading the type of material that any college student should expect to encounter on any college campus.

The *New Republic*'s Jenny Jarvie has traced the genesis of trigger warnings to online chat rooms and message boards frequented by survivors of highly traumatising experiences like rape.[3] In her March 2014 article 'Trigger Happy', Jarvie noted that the warnings, which 'began as a way of moderating internet forums for the vulnerable and mentally ill', spread through feminist forums like wildfire, prompting writer Susannah Breslin to proclaim in April 2010 that feminists were using the term 'like a Southern cook applies Pam cooking spray to an overused nonstick frying pan'.[4] From there, the phenomenon mushroomed into a staggeringly broad advisory system that, as Jarvie explained, now covers 'topics as diverse as sex, pregnancy, addiction, bullying, suicide, sizeism, ableism, homophobia, transphobia, slut-shaming, victim-blaming, alcohol, blood, insects, small holes and animals in wigs'. In May 2012, the *Awl*'s Choire Sicha penned an article titled 'When "Trigger Warning" Lost All Its Meaning'.[5] In it, Sicha discussed 'how far afield "trigger warnings" have gone', calling the trend 'insulting' and 'infantilising'.

Despite such criticism, trigger warnings are gaining traction – and are no longer confined to internet forums. The leap from online communities to college campuses is not surprising, as campuses have long been at the vanguard of accommodating student, faculty and administrator demands for emotionally and intellectually comfortable environments. Some believe that campuses have a duty to shield students from difficult material, while others espouse the older view, popularised by colleges like Yale in the 1970s, that colleges should be places where students are encouraged to 'think the unthinkable, discuss the unmentionable and challenge the unchallengeable'.[6] This contrast is stark and has certainly unsettled many professors.[7]

In early 2014, Oberlin College took a dramatic step toward heightening students' intellectual comfort by posting a trigger-warning policy on its website. Although the policy did not mandate the use of trigger warnings, it heavily encouraged the faculty to employ them as a means of 'making classrooms safer'.

It is crucial, at this point, to note how thoroughly the definition of *safety* has been watered down on campus. The term is no longer limited to physical security – far from it. In my career, I have repeatedly seen *safety* conflated with *comfort* or even *reassurance*. It is hard for me to overemphasise how dangerous this shift is. Our society appears to have forgotten the moral of the fable 'The Boy Who Cried Wolf'. When there is confusion as to whether *safety* refers to protection from physical harm or mere discomfort, how can professors and administrators quickly assess the danger of a situation and make appropriate decisions to safeguard the physical security of their students? Making sure that such important words do not lose their meaning through inappropriately distorted usage is an essential part of fighting the movement towards freedom from speech.

Oberlin's policy – which was quickly tabled when panicked professors found out about it – shows how expansive and invasive trigger warnings can be.[8] Its stated purpose was to protect students suffering from PTSD due to sexual assault, but its list of potentially triggering topics extended far beyond sexual or physical abuse. Professors were asked to 'understand that sexual misconduct is inextricably tied to issues of privilege and oppression', and to therefore consider how topics like 'racism, classism, sexism, heterosexism, cissexism, ableism and other issues of privilege and oppression' could affect their students.

The breadth of this list reveals that trigger-warning policies often have little to do with the needs of actual PTSD sufferers. Bear in mind that PTSD is the current evolution of the term 'shell shock', which was developed after the First World War to describe long-term psychological harm due to sustained exposure to horrific experiences during wartime. In the 1970s, PTSD became the preferred term for referring to the condition of traumatised veterans of the Vietnam War. The term has tremendous emotional force, but its use in the trigger-warning debate is yet another troubling employment of an important word. What colleges like Oberlin describe as PTSD bears little resemblance to its original meaning, which focused on the results of exposure to severe and often prolonged physical violence, atrocities or other life-threatening or terrifying events. Survivors of sexual assault have experienced the type of trauma that fits this definition, but it is hard to see how people who have merely been exposed to 'classism' – something that virtually anyone can claim to have encountered in some way at some point – can be put in the same category.

Oberlin is not alone. Around the time that Oberlin was instituting its trigger-warning policy, the student government at the University of California, Santa Barbara (UCSB) passed a 'Resolution to Mandate Warnings for Triggering Content in Academic Settings', which the UCSB administration is currently in the process of implementing.[9] The resolution provides a 'suggested list of trigger warnings [that] includes rape, sexual assault, abuse, self-injurious behaviour, suicide, graphic violence, pornography, kidnapping and graphic depictions of gore'.

Bailey Loverin, the student who co-authored the UCSB resolution, was inspired to do so after watching a film depicting rape in class. Although she identifies as a survivor of sexual abuse, she has specifically stated that she 'was not triggered by [her] classroom experience'.[10] Rather, she found it 'disturbing and sickening'. In other words, she felt highly uncomfortable while watching the film. The rules of political correctness seem to counsel against responding with the real answer: that college is where you are supposed to learn about the world as it truly is, which includes covering some horrific and dreadful topics. This endeavour should make anyone with a conscience uncomfortable at times, but that discomfort is a necessary part of real, adult-level education.

A quick look at recent campus dustups gives a more complete understanding of what the results of trigger-warning policies will be.

In February 2014, students at Wellesley College were outraged when an artist placed a statue of a man sleepwalking in his underwear on campus.[11] There is nothing overtly sexual or threatening about the statue, which was erected as part of a sculpture exhibit. If anything, the sleepwalker seems vulnerable: his eyes are closed, he is unaware of his surroundings and he is barely dressed. Despite this, students called it 'a source of apprehension, fear, and triggering thoughts regarding sexual assault for many members of our campus community' in a Change.org petition seeking its removal.[12]

One of the most powerful aspects of art is its capacity to provoke thought and debate, often by raising some hackles. Yet Zoe Magid, who started the petition, asserted that artwork that makes people uncomfortable has no place at Wellesley: 'We really feel that if a piece of art makes students feel unsafe, that steps over a line.'[13] Make sure to note how *unsafe* is used in this context.

At UCSB (again), a professor used the idea of triggers to defend getting into a physical altercation with campus protesters.[14] In March 2014, Mireille Miller-Young, a UCSB feminist-studies professor, spotted a young woman carrying a pro-life sign that displayed images of aborted fetuses. She tore the sign from the activist's hands and went so far as to shove another protester who tried to retrieve it. When questioned by the UCSB Police Department, Miller-Young – who was pregnant at the time – declared that 'she felt "triggered" by the images on the poster'. She also portrayed herself as a defender of student comfort, claiming that 'other students in the area were "triggered" in a negative way by their imagery'. In other words, she placed greater value on the emotional comfort of those with whom she identified than on the physical security of the woman she assaulted. In the video of the incident, Miller-Young seems positively gleeful to have taken the protester's sign, and her actions make her argument that she was personally triggered, as opposed to simply angry, difficult to believe.[15] That defence appears to be little more than a *post hoc* way of making her seem more sympathetic.

It is easy to dismiss events like this as rare acts of lunacy. One can argue that Miller-Young was just a lone professor making a transparent attempt to garner sympathy for – or otherwise excuse – illegal behaviour. It is also easy to dismiss the rising popularity of trigger warnings as a flash in the pan that will fade in the face of public ridicule. Yet the policies and confrontations that stem from the concept of trigger warnings are just further symptoms of the increasing expectations of intellectual comfort and freedom from speech on campus. While it is possible that the particular problem of demands for trigger warnings will be short-lived (though I doubt it), there will persist a larger problem where outsiders are made responsible for safeguarding the emotional state of all, even at the risk of impeding discourse on dead-serious topics that must be explored.

The UCSB case also highlights how such policies will inevitably be abused. An unfortunate truth of human nature is that if we are given a cudgel that may be wielded against people and views we oppose, some of us will gladly swing it. I can say with near 100 per cent confidence that students and even other faculty members will use trigger rationales to silence voices on campus that they merely dislike.

Professors know it is already shockingly easy to get in trouble for what you say at today's colleges. Take the 2014 example of art instructor Francis Schmidt of Bergen Community College in New Jersey, who was suspended without pay and ordered to undergo psychological counselling for posting on Google Plus a picture of his daughter wearing a t-shirt featuring a quote from the warrior queen Daenerys Targaryen, a character on HBO's mega-hit *Game of Thrones*: 'I will take what is mine with fire and blood.'[16] Depressingly, the quote was interpreted by administrators as a serious threat of violence. A security official even claimed that the 'fire' reference could be a proxy for the gunfire of an AK-47. A strikingly similar case, this time involving a quote from the sci-fi cult television classic *Firefly*, took place at the University of Wisconsin-Stout in 2011.[17]

Broaching sex-related topics in the classroom can be particularly risky, with professors at Appalachian State University,[18] the University of Colorado, Boulder[19] and the University of Colorado, Denver[20] all facing harassment charges and removal from teaching for the inclusion of sexual content in their class materials and discussions, even though the content was demonstrably relevant to each course.

In an environment like this, imposing on professors the duty to anticipate and be responsible for their students' emotional reactions to material will simply create new rationales for students or administrators seeking to punish provocative instructors. Such an expectation would be disastrous for teaching and would place professors in an impossible position.

Oberlin professor Marc Blecher has pointed out that instructors without tenure would be particularly vulnerable to this effect, telling the *New York Times*, 'If I were a junior faculty member looking at this [the Oberlin policy] while putting my syllabus together, I'd be terrified'.[21] In May 2014, seven humanities professors from seven colleges penned an *Inside Higher Ed* article stating that 'this movement is already having a chilling effect on [their] teaching and pedagogy'.[22] They reported receiving 'phone calls from deans and other administrators investigating student complaints that they have included "triggering" material in their courses, with or without warnings'. Sometime in the not-so-distant future – if it has not happened already – professors *will* be punished for not providing a trigger warning before discussing material that a student finds objectionable.

The seven professors also raised an important point about how trigger-warning policies may well harm, rather than help, the very students they claim to protect: 'Trigger warnings may encourage students to file claims against faculty rather than seek support and resources for debilitating reactions to stressors.' Students with PTSD are suffering from a serious mental-health condition and should seek professional assistance for it. In her article 'Treatment, Not Trigger Warnings', Sarah Roff, a psychiatrist who specialises in the mental effects of trauma (including flashbacks and panic attacks), explained that training students to avoid certain topics can be quite detrimental:

> One of the cardinal symptoms of PTSD is avoidance, which can become the most impairing symptom of all. If someone has been so affected by an event in her life that reading a description of a rape in Ovid's *Metamorphoses* can trigger nightmares, flashbacks and panic attacks, she is likely to be functionally impaired in areas of her life well beyond the classroom. The solution is not to help these students dig themselves further into a life of fear and avoidance.[23]

Proponents of trigger warnings argue that safeguarding the comfort of traumatised students is well worth the potential costs. Their position holds great emotional appeal. In the words of *Shakesville*'s Melissa McEwan, a leading trigger-warning advocate, 'We provide trigger warnings because it's polite, because we don't want to be the asshole who triggered a survivor of sexual assault because of carelessness or laziness or ignorance'.[24] The vast majority of us don't want to hurt others, particularly those who have already been badly hurt.

This emotional appeal can serve as a formidable weapon. Those who oppose trigger warnings are accused of being insensitive to the needs of vulnerable groups. It is also considered illegitimate to question the sincerity of emotional responses, which makes it easy for students who dislike certain ideas (or individuals) to try to silence them by claiming to have been triggered by them. Casting doubt on such an assertion would constitute 'victim-blaming', which only a coldhearted monster would do.[25] Alleging that someone is insensitive to the emotional state of victims is a powerful and effective shortcut to taking the moral high ground in contemporary debate.

The fear of being demonised in this manner is justified, given the power of the modern 'Twittermob' and other manifestations of popular outrage. In fact, such concerns are particularly valid on campus, where professors rightfully fear for their jobs if they manage to spark the moral indignation of some subset of students, administrators or faculty members. It is for this reason that groups that fight for professors' rights, such as my organisation, the Foundation for Individual Rights in Education (FIRE), and the American Association of University Professors (AAUP), must do their best to bolster professorial resistance to new and impossible expectations like trigger warnings. Otherwise, we risk squandering the opportunity to work with our natural allies (in this case at least) – university professors – to oppose the push toward elevating intellectual comfort over intellectual growth.

In rereading the commentary and reactions to the *New York Times* article that I mentioned at the beginning of this chapter, I noticed that defenders of trigger warnings often struck a common note. Essentially, they argued, 'What's the big deal? So you have to include two little words before you cover emotionally difficult material. Is it really that much to ask?' I have offered various answers to that question throughout this chapter, but, in conclusion, I want to stress two of them. First, the trouble with trigger warnings lies less in the individual practice (although it will present a huge problem for teaching) than in what that practice represents. Trigger warnings starkly reinforce the mentality that demands freedom *from* speech. Second, the trigger-warning issue is a genuinely slippery slope, as Oberlin's staggeringly broad policy demonstrates.

Supporters of trigger warnings are sometimes shocked by the negative response that the idea, as applied to college content, has received in the press and the blogosphere. For those who believe that offering such warnings is simply a means of showing empathy, conscientiousness and care, the widespread criticism of the practice is probably fairly mystifying. To those who value intellectual freedom, however, trigger warnings are yet another manifestation of the attitude that society must protect every individual from emotionally difficult speech. It is impossible to live up to this expectation, and, in the course of trying to do so, we risk devastating freedom of speech and the open exchange of ideas.

Critics might dismiss my and others' concerns about what trigger warnings represent as a slippery-slope fallacy. But if there is one thing that I have discovered in fighting for free speech on campus, it is that, when it comes to limitations on speech and the uniquely sensitive environment of college campuses, the slope is genuinely perilously slick.

In my career, I have seen harassment rationales – meant to prevent misogynists from forcing women out of jobs through constant abuse – being invoked to justify censoring everything from quoting popular television shows[26] to faintly implying criticism of a university's hockey coach[27] to publicly reading a book.[28] The slippery slope of censorship is demonstrably not a fallacy on campus. When students take advantage of a psychological term developed to help those traumatised in the ghastly trenches of the First World War to justify being protected from *The Great Gatsby*, sleepwalker statues and, as the Oberlin policy specified, Chinua Achebe,[29] it becomes clear that there is virtually no limit to the demands that will be made if we universalise an expectation of intellectual comfort.

Other critics see where this is headed, as well. As Professor Roff wrote in the article mentioned above, 'since triggers are a contagious phenomenon, there will never be enough trigger warnings to keep up with them'.[30] And as Conor Friedersdorf wrote in the *Atlantic*:

> The future before us if the most sweeping plans for 'trigger warnings' become reality, is a kind of arms race, where different groups of students demand that their highly particular, politicised sensitivities are as deserving of a trigger warning as any other. Everyone from anarchists to college Republicans will join in. Kids will feel trauma when their trauma isn't recognised as trauma. 'Trigger warnings' will be as common and useless as 'adult content' warnings on HBO.
> Everyone will be worse off.[31]

Friedersdorf is right. Trigger warnings push the bar ever lower for what is deemed unacceptably offensive, while the realm of unacceptable speech grows ever larger. This is a global race to the bottom, and it is being run most fiercely in higher education. In the process, candour, discussion, humour, honest dialogue and freedom of speech are imperilled.

Greg Lukianoff *is the president of the Foundation for Individual Rights in Education (FIRE) and the author of* Unlearning Liberty *and* Freedom From Speech.

Notes

This chapter is an excerpt from *Freedom From Speech*, which is published by Encounter Books.

1. 'Warning: The Literary Canon Could Make Students Squirm', *New York Times*, 17 May 2014, nytimes.com/2014/05/18/us/warning-the-literary-canon-could-make-students-squirm.html?_r=1.
2. 'Trigger warnings needed in classroom', by Philip Wythe, *Daily Targum*, 18 February 2014, dailytargum.com/article/2014/02/trigger-warnings-needed-in-classroom.
3. 'Trigger Happy', by Jennie Jarvey, *New Republic*, 3 March 2014, newrepublic.com/article/116842/trigger-warnings-have-spread-blogs-college-classes-thats-bad.
4. Quoted in: 'Trigger Happy', newrepublic.com/article/116842/trigger-warnings-have-spread-blogs-college-classes-thats-bad.
5. 'When "Trigger Warning" Lost All Its Meaning', by Choire Sicha, *Awl*, 30 May 2012, theawl.com/2012/05/when-trigger-warning-lost-all-its-meaning.
6. 'Freedom of Expression', Yale College, yalecollege.yale.edu/new-students/class-2019/academic-information/intro-undergrad-education/freedom-expression.
7. 'The Downside of Trigger Warnings', by Elwood Watson, *Diverse*, 27 May 2014, diverseeducation.com/article/64546/.
8. 'Trigger Unhappy', *Inside Higher Ed*, 14 April 2014, insidehighered.com/news/2014/04/14/oberlin-backs-down-trigger-warnings-professors-who-teach-sensitive-material.
9. 'A Resolution to Mandate Warnings For Triggering Content in Academic Settings', Associated Students Senate, University of California, Santa Barbara, ucsb.edu/senate/resolutions/a-resolution-to-mandate-warnings-for-triggering-content-in-academic-settings/.
10. 'Trigger Warnings at UCSB', by Bailey Loverin, *Daily Nexus*, 11 March 2014, dailynexus.com/2014-03-11/trigger-warnings-at-ucsb/.
11. 'Underwear-clad "Sleepwalker" statue at Wellesley College vandalised with yellow paint', *New York Daily News*, 22 May 2014, nydailynews.com/news/national/underwear-clad-sleepwalker-statue-wellesley-college-vandalized-yellow-paint-article-1.1802446.
12. 'Move the "Sleepwalker" Inside the David Museum', Change.org, 5 February 2014, change.org/p/president-h-kim-bottomly-move-the-sleepwalker-inside-the-davis-museum.
13. 'Realistic statue of man in his underwear at Wellesley College sparks controversy', Boston.com, 5 February 2014, boston.com/yourcampus/news/wellesley/2014/02/realistic_statue_of_man_in_his_underwear_at_wellesley_college_sparks_controversy.html.
14. 'Campus Trigger Warnings Threaten Speech and Treat Students Like Children', by Robert Shibley and Araz Shibley, *Reason*, 27 May 2014, reason.com/archives/2014/05/27/trigger-warnings-on-campus-arent-just-fu/1.
15. 'UC Santa Barbara Professor Assaults Young Pro-Life Activist', YouTube, 12 March 2014, youtube.com/watch?v=sLemX9QtUa4.
16. 'Borgen Administrators Fear "Game of Thrones" Quote, Censor Professor', *Torch*, 16 April 2014, thefire.org/bergen-administrators-fear-game-of-thrones-quote-censor-professor/.
17. 'How "Firefly" Fans Saved Free Speech on Campus', *Torch*, 28 December 2011, thefire.org/new-fire-video-how-firefly-fans-saved-free-speech-on-campus/.
18. 'Appalachian State University: Professor Suspended for Classroom Speech', FIRE, thefire.org/cases/appalachian-state-university-professor-suspended-for-classroom-speech/.

19. 'This Is What the Chilling Effect Looks Like: Acclaimed Classroom Skit at U. of Colorado Canceled', *Torch*, 9 April 2014, thefire.org/this-is-what-the-chilling-effect-looks-like-acclaimed-classroom-skit-at-u-of-colorado-canceled/.
20. 'University of Denver: Sexual Harassment Finding Violates Professor's Academic Freedom in the Classroom', FIRE, thefire.org/cases/university-of-denver-sexual-harassment-finding-violates-professors-academic-freedom-in-the-classroom/.
21. 'Warning: The Literary Canon Could Make Students Squirm', 2014, nytimes.com/2014/05/18/us/warning-the-literary-canon-could-make-students-squirm.html?_r=1.
22. 'Trigger Warnings Are Flawed', *Inside Higher Ed*, 29 May 2014, insidehighered.com/views/2014/05/29/essay-faculty-members-about-why-they-will-not-use-trigger-warnings#ixzz34YUzvJbK.
23. 'Treatment, Not Trigger Warnings', by Sarah Roff, *Chronicle of Higher Education*, 23 May 2014, chronicle.com/blogs/conversation/2014/05/23/treatment-not-trigger-warnings/.
24. '[Trigger warning.]', Melissa McEwan, Shakesville.com, 13 April 2010, shakesville.com/2010/04/i-write-letters_13.html.
25. 'Social Scientist Sees Bias Within', by John Tierney, *New York Times*, 7 February 2011, nytimes.com/2011/02/08/science/08tier.html?_r=0.
26. 'Neil Gaiman Talks Firefly, Free Speech On Campus, and One of the Craziest Cases of the Year (VIDEO)', by Greg Lukianoff, *Huffington Post*, 29 December 2011, huffingtonpost.com/greg-lukianoff/neil-gaiman-talks-firefly_b_1171945.html.
27. 'SUNY Oswego Journalism Student Suspended for Emails to Hockey Coaches', *Torch*, 9 November 2012, thefire.org/suny-oswego-journalism-student-suspended-for-emails-to-hockey-coaches/.
28. 'Indiana University – Purdue University Indianapolis: Student Employee Found Guilty of "Racial Harassment" for Reading a Book', FIRE, thefire.org/cases/indiana-university-purdue-university-indianapolis-student-employee-found-guilty-of-racial-harassment-for-reading-a-book/.
29. 'We've gone too far with "trigger warnings"', by Jill Filipovic, *Guardian*, 5 March 2014, theguardian.com/commentisfree/2014/mar/05/trigger-warnings-can-be-counterproductive.
30. 'Treatment, Not Trigger Warnings', by Sarah Roff, *Chronicle of Higher Education*, 23 May 2014, chronicle.com/blogs/conversation/2014/05/23/treatment-not-trigger-warnings/.
31. 'What HBO Can Teach Colleges About "Trigger Warnings"', by Conor Friedersdorf, *Atlantic*, 20 May 2014, theatlantic.com/education/archive/2014/05/what-trigger-warning-activists-and-critics-can-learn-from-hbo/371137/.

6

BDS: Demonising Israel, Destroying Free Speech

Sean Collins

The Boycott, Divestment and Sanctions (BDS) movement is a campaign that seeks to put pressure on Israel to adopt its stated aims, which include 'ending its occupation and colonialisation of all Arab lands', 'recognising the fundamental rights of the Arab-Palestinian citizens of Israel to full equality', and 'respecting, protecting and promoting the rights of Palestinian refugees to return to their homes and properties'.[1] The BDS movement has gained much notoriety in the US, UK and elsewhere in recent years, and universities are particularly important sites for its activities.

BDS seeks to delegitimise Israel, and advocates censoring anyone connected with Israel. Of course, anyone should be free to criticise Israel's policies, BDS included. At the same time, it must be recognised that BDS is inherently hostile to free speech. It is not a stretch to say that these anti-Israel campaigners are the most censorious group on campuses today.

For those who support the exchange of ideas, BDS's increasing prominence raises the question of how best to defend free speech when it comes to the issue of Israel and the Palestinians. As I argue here, some of the more high-profile cases of opposing BDS have been misguided, in that they have sought to clamp down on BDS in illiberal ways – in other words, they have stooped to BDS's own censorious level. It would be much better and effective, in my view, to respond with a principled stand for freedom of speech.

The rise of BDS

According to BDS, its campaign originated in 2005, when 171 Palestinian organisations called for action against Israel. However, as Cary Nelson notes, the first of today's BDS actions in the US began earlier, in 2002, with a campaign calling on the University of California to divest in companies that allegedly benefitted from a relationship with Israel.[2] BDS has since grown via the activities of supportive organisations, including the US Campaign for the Academic and Cultural Boycott of Israel (USACBI) and Students for Justice in Palestine (SJP), which has about 100 campus chapters in the US.

Of BDS's three methods, 'boycott' is the most prominent. 'Divestment' campaigns are fairly common at universities – for example, student governments at six University of California campuses have passed resolutions calling for divestment from Israel – but most fail to convince the university to divest (although they could be considered successful in raising the profile and arguments of BDS). 'Sanctions' campaigns are less of a focus for BDS, and less successful, as they require persuading national governments to take action.

As part of its 'boycott' initiatives, BDS encourages economic boycotts of Israel – such as urging consumers not to buy Israeli products – but these have had very little effect. As one report points out, 95 per cent of Israeli exports are to other businesses, not consumers.[3] Student groups like to boycott Sabra hummus, but that company represents a tiny proportion of Israel's economy.

When it comes to boycott campaigns, BDS devotes more energy to its boycotts of academic and cultural events and people than it does to stopping Israeli products. BDS seeks to prevent Israeli academics from speaking and collaborating with other academics outside Israel, including academic conferences, intellectual collaborations and research projects. Similarly, it seeks to prevent Israeli artists from performing in the US and other places outside Israel, and calls on Western artists to not perform in Israel. In other words, if it had its way, BDS and its supporters would prevent Israeli academics and artists from engaging with us at all.

The cultural boycotts have had mixed success. Thanks to pressure from BDS, musicians Elvis Costello and Roger Waters have cancelled performances in Israel. In 2012, writer Alice Walker refused to authorise a Hebrew translation of her novel, *The Color Purple*. And, in 2013, physicist Stephen Hawking, following calls from BDS, decided not to attend a conference in Israel. But for every Costello and Waters there have been other musicians – including Elton John, Madonna, the Rolling Stones and Justin Bieber – who have refused to kowtow to demands to cancel tours. And, in 2014, actress Scarlett Johansson told BDS where to go when she declined to stop advertising for Sodastream, an Israeli company.

BDS wages war on academic freedom

It is in the academy where the debate on BDS is most heated, and arguably where BDS has the most potential to have a detrimental effect.

The boycotts of Israeli academics and universities first took off in the
UK, led by professors sympathetic to BDS. In 2002, professors Hilary
and Steven Rose wrote an open letter to the *Guardian*, calling for a
moratorium on links with Israeli institutions; 700 academics signed. In
2005, the council of the Association of University Teachers (AUT) voted
to boycott two Israeli universities: the University of Haifa and Bar-Ilan
University (later that year, a special meeting of the AUT overturned
the vote). In 2006, the National Association of Teachers in Further and
Higher Education (NATFHE) passed a motion to boycott Israeli academics who did not oppose their government. In 2011, the University and
College Union (created by the merger of the AUT and NATFHE) voted to
adopt an academic and cultural boycott of Israel. All of these decisions
were met with criticism.

In the US, the biggest move towards breaking academic ties with Israel
came in 2013, when the American Studies Association (ASA) voted to
boycott Israeli academic institutions. This led to a controversial public
debate, with many university presidents and other organisations condemning the vote, including the American Council on Education (ACE),
the Association of American Universities (AAU), and the American
Association of University Professors (AAUP).

Boycotts have had a real impact in the academy: Israeli academics
have been removed from the editorial boards of journals; PhD students
have been turned down for scholarships; academics have been denied
speaking slots at conferences; and so on. But even in cases where votes
or statements have had only symbolic effects, they nonetheless cast a
chill over campus discussion of Israel and the Palestinians.

Clearly, if BDS had its way, the academic world would become a
complete no-speech zone when it comes to Israelis. Omar Barghouti is
co-founder of the Palestinian Campaign for the Academic and Cultural
Boycott of Israel (PACBI), and one of the leading campaigners calling for
a boycott of Israeli academics. According to Barghouti, Israeli academics
are 'complicit' with 'a system of oppression' in Israel. Along with his
co-author, Lisa Taraki, he has written dismissively about academic freedom for Israeli academics:

> We think that the freedom that Israeli academics appear keen to pre-
> serve is the freedom to continue being scholars – that is, to have an

uninterrupted flow of research funds, to continue to get grants to be released from teaching, to take sabbaticals, to continue to be able to write, engage in scholarly debate, and to do all the things respectable academics are supposed to do. But can they or should they be able to enjoy these freedoms (which sound more like privileges to us) without any regard to what is going on outside of the walls of the academy, to the role of their institutions in the perpetuation of colonial rule?[4]

In fact, Barghouti has been explicit in stating that Israeli academics should be denied the normal rights that other academics enjoy. When the AAUP adopted a stance against academic boycotts, Barghouti responded by writing: 'When scholars neglect or otherwise abandon said obligations, they thereby forfeit their right to exercise academic freedom.'[5]

The American arm of BDS, USACBI, is equally explicit about denying academics the right to collaborate with Israeli academics. Historically, the exchange of ideas has led to intellectual progress and social benefits – but USACBI is having none of that when it comes to Israel: 'Ultimately, the exchange of ideas does not necessarily make a difference that results in a more humane world or more humane outlooks.' It adds: 'All academic exchanges with Israeli academics do have the effect of normalising Israel and its politics of occupation and apartheid.'[6] The BDS campaign would prefer to delegitimise those who support Israel and its policies, proclaiming 'there is no debate', because then it wouldn't have to marshal arguments and persuade people.

BDS claims that it should be free to call on Western academics and universities to cut ties with Israeli individuals and institutions. USACBI says: 'Supporting the academic boycott is an exercise of academic freedom.'[7] Yes, BDS-supporting academics should be free to say whatever they like. However, make no mistake: they are using their speech to try to restrict others' freedoms of expression and association – an exercise in denying academic freedom to others. The AAUP puts it well: universities should be 'institutions committed to the search for truth and its free expression'.[8] But BDS believes in the opposite: that academic freedom is contingent on the political views of the individual.

BDS on campus: stifling debate

BDS's declaration that Israeli academics are beyond the pale has gene-rated a wider sense among the movement that it should adopt a zero-tolerance attitude towards all things related to Israel on campuses. In particular, this seems to give BDS a self-justification for clamping down on debate on the issue of Israel. As BDS's outlook is entirely infused with a desire to silence pro-Israel figures, it is not surprising that their supporters seek to curtail free speech in its day-to-day activities on university grounds.

There are many cases in recent years where Israeli politicians, military figures and other representatives have been shouted down at speaking events across the US (as well as in other countries, especially the UK). In a well-publicised case, students at the University of California, Irvine orchestrated disruptions of a speech by Michael Oren, the Israeli ambassador, in 2010. This disruption was supported by the USACBI, which has received endorsements from over 800 academics across the US. In his authoritative book on censorship on American campuses, *Unlearning Liberty*, Greg Lukianoff describes the scene in Irvine that day:

> UC Irvine officials repeatedly came up and explained that this behaviour was against the university's policies, that it was an attempt to disrupt a speech, and that students who continued would be punished. The students did continue, however, culminating in the ambassador having to stop the speech and return later, once again to be met with repeated attempts to shout him down. The group, somewhat ironically, finally staged a mass exit before the question-and-answer period – the time when students could have challenged Oren directly.[9]

This act of disruption was indicative of how supporters of BDS operate today. First, they do not wish to listen to or engage in debate – as evidenced by the unwillingness to ask questions. USACBI called on its supporters to send a message to the university's administrators: 'It is not the mission of the UC [University of California] system to provide an uncritical venue for the ambassador of Israel to spread his political message.' But it was not an uncritical venue – even though the disruptive students were trying to make it so.

Next, BDS often claims that it is a victim, that its free-speech rights have somehow been infringed, as it did following the Irvine incident. But as Lukianoff notes: 'This was an orchestrated act of civil disobedience that was hostile to the value of free and open discourse, not supportive of it ... Too many students seem to believe they have a free-speech right to take over or in some cases completely shut down speech they dislike.'

For pro-Israel students in the UK, being shouted down or told to shut up is a common experience. When the London School of Economics invited Israeli ambassador Daniel Taub to speak in February 2015, protesters blocked students from entering, and set off the fire alarm during the talk.[10] Reporting for *spiked*, Tom Slater described what happened at King's College London in 2014, when an event organised by the KCL Israel Society was disrupted by students' union staff:

> Picture the scene. A university society has organised an event on campus involving an external speaker. Then, despite following the bureaucratic students' union procedure for getting the event approved, the society receives notification two days before the event is due to take place that it has been 'flagged' as controversial. Further measures, the society is told, will be required for it to be signed off. After various squabbles between society and SU over the format and provisions for the event, it goes ahead uncensored. But, as the event is about to get underway, the SU's 'Safe Space officer' bowls down. He appoints himself doorman. He stops certain students from entering. At one point, he asks the speaker to leave. And it culminates in him squaring off with the event's organiser, leaving him cowed and humiliated.[11]

As Slater notes, when it comes to UK universities: 'Nothing is more likely to bring out the student censors, the intolerant monitors of campus life and thought, than the issue of Israel. You want to say something positive about Israel on a UK campus? Then you do so at your own peril.'

As in academia, BDS also tries to shut down cultural expressions in other venues. Performances by Israeli groups are regularly targeted by BDS protesters. Batsheva, the Israeli dance troupe, encountered such protests in 2012 in the US. A sympathetic report painted the picture: 'Calling on attendees to boycott Batsheva due to its complicity with Israeli human-rights violations, activists sang, chanted, played music, and danced. Parodying a piece of Batsheva's newest show, *Hora*, [New York anti-Israel group] Adalah-NY was joined by the Columbia University Palestinian Dabke Brigades and the Rude Mechanical Orchestra in a costumed *Star Wars*-themed dance representing the struggle between good and evil ...'[12] Noise from the protesters delayed the performance.

Some might think that dancers have little to do with Israeli government policy, or politics generally. But according to BDS protesters, this dance troupe needs to adopt political positions and 'take a stand against the human-rights violations being perpetuated by its government'.

Barghouti justifies the targeting of Batsheva on the basis that the troupe operates at 'an even deeper level of complicity. Those same dancers are part-time occupation soldiers … killing children and letting pregnant women die at checkpoints.'[13]

The claim that Israeli academics and artists are 'complicit' is bogus. Academia and culture should be arenas to discuss issues, not shut them down due to disagreement. Israeli academics and artists are not responsible for their government's policies. There is a double standard at work here. Would you require American institutions – such as Columbia University, the National Institutes of Health or the New York Philharmonic – to produce political statements, say to denounce American intervention in Iraq and Afghanistan? Of course not.

Creating an atmosphere of anti-Semitism

Criticism of Israel's policies is not anti-Semitic. But BDS does more than criticise Israeli policy. There are two key features which make BDS anti-Semitic in effect, even if its supporters have no intention of being such: the singling-out of Israel, and the expansion of the boycott campaign to Israeli culture.

In the BDS worldview, Israel is identified as uniquely wicked. This is deeply problematic: one can name many repressive regimes around the world, many of them in the Middle East, that have less regard for human rights than Israel does, and yet BDS supporters want us to focus exclusively on Israel. Why not boycott other countries? How about the US, perhaps, which is a far bigger power player in the Middle East than Israel? 'The situation is different' in the US, says USACBI, because 'millions of US citizens vigorously protested US militarism in the Middle East', which 'contributed to the election of Obama'. Oh yes, the same Obama who pursued wars in Iraq and Afghanistan, who engaged in new warfare in Libya, and whose regime has massively increased drone attacks in Afghanistan and Pakistan, killing thousands, including civilians. That's different.

In targeting Israeli academics and cultural performers, BDS imposes a form of collective punishment on the Israeli people. And in blaming all Israelis for the actions of the State of Israel, BDS promotes an anti-Semitic outlook in society. At the University of California, Los Angeles (UCLA), animosity towards Israel has spilled over into instances of hostility towards Jews. For example, UCLA's student council voted against the nomination of Jewish student Rachel Beyda to its judicial board on the grounds that her faith meant she was inherently biased.[14] Such is the atmosphere BDS has fostered.

An unhelpful response to BDS

It would be fair to say that BDS gets as good as it gives. On many college campuses, there are sizeable groups of academics and students who have criticised and protested against BDS's campaigns. And outside the university, there are a number of constituencies that are vocal opponents of BDS.

However, there has been a tendency, in the US and elsewhere, for BDS's adversaries to express their own form of intolerance in response to BDS. Such moves against BDS have been generally counterproductive: they give BDS the oxygen of publicity and, ironically, can make BDS appear to be the victim of an anti-free speech campaign. Let's consider three recent examples from North America: the attempt to cancel a BDS meeting at Brooklyn College; the reversal of hiring a professor, Steven Salaita, who is a BDS supporter; and legislative moves to 'boycott the boycotters' – that is, to apply penalties to BDS.

Brooklyn College

In 2013, members of New York City Council sent a letter to the president of Brooklyn College, denouncing the college's political science department for co-sponsoring a speaking event with supporters of the BDS movement. The council members' criticisms were backed by a threat to withdraw funding to the college (which it had the power to do, as Brooklyn College is part of the state City University of New York, or CUNY, system).

The officials' letter caused uproar, and various individuals proceeded to speak out for and against Brooklyn College's decision to host two BDS speakers – the BDS leader Barghouti, and Judith Butler, an academic who supports BDS. A slanging match broke out, with each side ratcheting up the rhetoric: Alan Maisel, a state assemblyman, said the event would represent a 'second Holocaust' if the college endorsed it, while the supporters of the political-science department referred to opponents' 'smear tactics and campaign of intimidation'.

In response, college president Karen Gould asserted the college's right to hold the event on the grounds of academic freedom. A *New York Times* editorial came out against the council members,[15] and then New York mayor Michael Bloomberg issued a robust attack on government interference in the academy:

> Well look, I couldn't disagree more violently with BDS, as they call it. As you know, I'm a big supporter of Israel, as big a one as you can

find in the city, but I could also not agree more strongly with an academic department's right to sponsor a forum on any topic that they choose. I mean, if you want to go to a university where the government decides what kinds of topics are fit for discussion, I suggest you apply to a school in North Korea.[16]

One by one, council members started to withdraw their opposition, and the storm subsided. The BDS debate went ahead, without any major hitches.

The calls from government officials to pressure Brooklyn College to cancel the event were clearly wrong, and a violation of free speech. The BDS group's specific views do not matter in this respect: even though some people may find its views offensive, BDS should be free to air them, and a college should be free to invite it to do so. As Bloomberg noted, the freedom to discuss issues – including controversial opinions held by a minority of people – is at the heart of academic life. Brooklyn College should not have been put under pressure, and there should be complete academic freedom in this regard.

The opposition to the BDS event amounted to a very heavy-handed and clumsy attempt by a relatively small number of politicians to interfere with a college campus event. It was widely recognised as such, and the would-be pro-Israel censors never gained much wider public support. In the event, their hyped-up opposition backfired on them, as the furore ended up giving BDS more publicity than it would have otherwise received.

However, amid all of the poses struck in defence of academic freedom, what was less recognised and commented on during the Brooklyn College fuss was the fact that BDS itself is thoroughly censorious. There was an irony that went right over the heads of the supporters of the event: they were fighting a free-speech campaign in favour of a group that is completely against free speech.

Steven Salaita

Steven Salaita is an American academic and prominent BDS advocate. In 2013, the University of Illinois offered Salaita a position, to begin in August 2014. However, shortly before he was due to start, the chancellor, Phyllis Wise, decided not to take his appointment to the university's board of trustees for approval, thus effectively withdrawing the job offer. It was then revealed that Wise and the trustees had received hundreds of complaints from donors and alumni about the many anti-Israel comments Salaita had made on Twitter, as well as his BDS activism. Salaita demanded to be reinstated, but the board voted against reconsidering the offer.

Many of Salaita's comments on Twitter could be considered unprofessional and uncivil. Some were downright anti-Semitic: 'If Netanyahu appeared on TV with a necklace made from the teeth of Palestinian children, would anyone be surprised? #Gaza.'

But despite the problematic nature of Salaita's comments, the University of Illinois was wrong to withdraw its job offer. He had been approved unanimously by the faculty, and the board's approval is nearly always a formality. Moreover, professors should be allowed freedom to express their views – and that includes on Twitter, and in an uncivil manner. The university sent a bad message about its tolerance of thought and speech on campus when it rescinded its offer to Salaita.

Salaita made it clear that he believes his academic freedom had been violated. He's correct: the university did trample on his rights. However, if you read Salaita's earlier writings, you find that he was not all that wild about free speech before this incident; he has stated that he is 'tepid about academic freedom as a right'.[17] That was before he accepted money from the AAUP to fight his case on the grounds of academic freedom. He also, as mentioned, is at the forefront of trying to deny academic freedom to Israeli academics. So, it turns out that what Salaita really believes in is privileged speech: he and other like-minded professors should be allowed to say what they want, but Israeli lecturers and researchers shouldn't, because they have the wrong views.

That makes Salaita a hypocrite. But the university, by treating him in such a brusque and inept way, turned him into a martyr in some people's eyes. Worse still, Salaita became identified as a defender of free speech.

'Boycott the boycotters'

In response to BDS, legislatures in the US and Canada have drafted bills designed to curtail BDS's influence. In May 2015, Illinois's House of Representatives joined the state Senate in passing a so-called 'anti-BDS' bill, which prohibits the state's pension fund from investing in companies that boycott Israel. Illinois is the first US state to adopt such legislation, but others are said to be considering it.

There are similar anti-BDS moves in process at the federal level. Bipartisan amendments to the US congressional bills for the Trade Promotion Authority include a call to discourage boycotts as one of the US's goals in trade negotiations. Another proposed national bill is the 'Boycott Our Enemies, Not Israel Act', which requires government contractors to confirm they are not boycotting Israel.

In 2015, the Canadian government considered using hate-crime laws against groups that promoted boycotts of Israel. Steven Blaney, then Canada's public-security minister, said the government would take a 'zero tolerance' approach to BDS. Such a move could ensnare a variety of organisations, including church groups, unions and student associations.

In both the US and Canada, BDS has cried foul, claiming it's a victim of censorship. This is rich coming from a group whose *raison d'être* is to silence Israelis and shut down debate, whether it is No Platforming a Zionist speaker at a college or campaigning to shut down an Israeli dance troupe. As *spiked*'s editor Brendan O'Neill has written, BDS types are 'the world's least convincing free-speech warriors'.[18] What they are really calling for is privileged protection for their own speech, not free speech for all.

That said, these legislative moves against BDS are misguided, even if BDS is hypocritical for crying censorship. Canada's hate-crime laws are an abomination for free speech, as they criminalise thought. As BDS is discovering, 'hate' is a nebulous concept that can be easily manipulated by the government in power. We should oppose the use of hate-speech laws in principle, regardless of whom they're aimed at.

The US does not (thankfully) have hate-speech laws, and the recent legislation against BDS is more limited in scope than that which was proposed in Canada. The new or proposed laws in the US do not ban participation in boycotts against Israel, nor do they prohibit advocating boycotts.

But even the more restricted US legislative measures are the wrong way to oppose BDS. Boycotting BDS is the mirror image of the politically correct call for 'zero tolerance towards intolerance'. Two wrongs don't make a right. In raising the threat of state retaliation against BDS, critics are giving some credence to BDS's overblown and hypocritical claims that it is being persecuted.

Taking a principled, free-speech stand against BDS

'We're witnessing the rise of a new McCarthyism in [the US] led by Israel, its lobby groups and defenders of the denial of basic Palestinian rights', said Barghouti, adopting the pose of the victim.[19] Certainly, BDS's opponents have played right into that view at times. But BDS shouldn't be allowed to get away with crying 'McCarthyism' when it faces opposition, given that it pursues its own blacklisting of an entire country's academics and artists. And the claim made by some BDS representatives that the academic boycott is aimed at institutions not individuals is pure semantics – institutions are made up of individuals, and opposing the 'institutions' means individuals become blacklisted.

Anyone who supports free speech – including those opposed to Israel's policies in the Middle East – should be against BDS-style censorship. We need to puncture the myth that BDS's boycott of Israel is somehow radical and progressive, and show how thoroughly anti-free speech it really is. Those who are serious about academic and artistic freedom should oppose both formal threats of censure from government bodies and informal campaigns that are waged against academics and artists.

And rather than 'boycott the boycotters', we need to argue for free speech for all. It is much better to allow BDS to make its case, and oppose its arguments openly. It's time to take the fight to the public arena, using ideas and arguments instead of boycotts and bans.

Sean Collins *is a writer based in New York and US correspondent for* spiked.

Notes

1. 'Palestinian Civil Society Call for BDS', bdsmovement.net, 9 July 2005, bds-movement.net/call.
2. 'Introduction', by Cary Nelson, In *The Case Against Academic Boycotts of Israel*, Cary Nelson and Gabriel Noah Brahm (eds), MLA Members for Scholars Rights, 2015.
3. 'Who's afraid of the big, bad boycott?', by Adam Reuter, Ynet News, 28 August 2014, ynetnews.com/articles/0,7340,L-4563597,00.html.
4. 'Academic Boycott and the Israeli Left', by Omar Barghouti and Lisa Taraki, *Electronic Intifada*, 15 April 2005, electronicintifada.net/content/academic-boycott-and-israeli-left/5550.
5. 'Critics of the AAUP report', by Omar Barghouti, In *Academic Boycotts: Conference Papers*, 2006, p. 44, aaup.org/file/Papers-From-A-Planned-Conference-on-Boycotts.pdf.
6. 'FAQs', US Campaign for the Academic and Cultural Boycott of Israel, usacbi. org/faqs/.
7. 'FAQs', usacbi.org/faqs/.
8. 'On Academic Boycotts', American Association of University Professors, aaup.org/report/academic-boycotts.
9. *Unlearning Liberty: Campus Censorship and the End of American Debate*, by Greg Lukianoff, Enounter Books, 2014, p. 228.
10. 'LSE probe praise for bomber', *Jewish Chronicle*, 5 February 2015, thejc.com/news/uk-news/129515/lse-probe-praise-bomber.
11. 'We don't feel welcome in our own universities', by Tom Slater, *spiked*, 18 December 2014, spiked-online.com/freespeechnow/fsn_article/we-dont-feel-welcome-in-our-own-universities#.VgqpLMtViko.

12. 'NY Activists Protest Israel's Batsheva Dance Company at Brooklyn Academy of Music', Adalah-NY, 7 March 2012, adalahny.org/press-release/881/ny-activists-protest-israel-batsheva-dance-company-brooklyn-academy-music.

13. 'No Dancing Around The Issues', by Eric Herschthal, US Campaign for the Academic and Cultural Boycott of Israel, usacbi.org/2009/03/no-dancing-around-the-issues/.

14. 'In UCLA Debate Over Jewish Student, Echoes on Campus of Old Biases', by Adam Nagourney, *New York Times*, 5 March 2015, nytimes.com/2015/03/06/us/debate-on-a-jewish-student-at-ucla.html.

15. 'Litmus tests', *New York Times*, 4 February 2013, nytimes.com/2013/02/05/opinion/litmus-tests-for-israel.html.

16. Quoted in: 'Debating Israel', *The Economist*, 7 February 2013, economist.com/blogs/democracyinamerica/2013/02/academic-freedom.

17. '*The Definition of Academic Freedom, for Many, Does Not Accommodate Dissent*', by Steven Salaita, University of Minnesota Press Blog, 16 April 2014, uminnpressblog.com/2014/04/the-definition-of-academic-freedom-for.html.

18. 'Anti-Israel academics: the world's least convincing free-speech warriors', by Brendan O'Neill, *spiked*, 31 March 2015, spiked-online.com/newsite/article/bononpalestine/16837#.VgqshMtViko.

19. 'Founder of anti-Israel BDS group calls out critics at Brooklyn College event; takes swipe at Mayor Bloomberg', *New York Daily News*, 7 February 2013, nydailynews.com/new-york/founder-anti-israel-group-calls-critics-brooklyn-college-event-article-1.1258500.

7

Debating Abortion on Campus: Let Both the Pro and Anti Sides Speak

Jon O'Brien

As an advocate of sexual and reproductive health, I greatly value the abil-ity to speak out and to raise issues, questions and concerns in the public square. I speak out in the hope that I can bring people closer to my per-spective, because I believe my perspective has the most to offer a free and democratic society. Naturally, there are some who disagree with my per-spective as a Catholic who believes that women and men must be free to follow their conscience on matters of sexual and reproductive healthcare and rights. I respect their right to disagree. While arguments can often feel uncomfortable, they are necessary and, indeed, healthy – especially if we want our communities to be places where no one is afraid of the battle of ideas. We can learn by listening to different perspectives in the forge of sometimes heated debate. Sadly, it seems that such a simple desire to have informed and diverse debate is increasingly the opposite of what is happening on college campuses across the US and the UK.

As a Catholic, I feel that restricting the free exchange of ideas at a university is contrary to the Catholic tradition of the university itself. The university, academic freedom and the Catholic Church have been intertwined since the Middle Ages. Medieval popes became champions of higher learning because the schools produced educated person-nel that the church needed. According to William J Hoye, a professor of systematic theology, Pope Honorius III was the first to articulate something like modern academic freedom. In 1220, this pope told the University of Bologna in Italy to defend its 'scholastic freedom' from the local government, which was trying to require students to take an oath of allegiance to the city. In 1231, Pope Gregory IX proved ahead of his time by granting the University of Paris the right to strike – against none other than the Bishop of Paris, who wanted control over the hir-ing and firing of professors.[1]

In the classroom, students enjoyed the freedom of inquiry which was in vogue. 'Yes, medieval scholars were concerned with accountability' to the church, theologian Jean Porter wrote in *Commonweal*, 'but they also defended freedom to conduct research and teaching as they saw fit'.[2]

It was a time 'when the intellect went wild, and had a licentious revel', said Blessed John Henry Newman of the late Middle Ages when universities were being established. 'When was there ever a more curious, more meddling, bolder, keener, more penetrating, more rationalistic exercise of reason than at that time?'[3]

Cardinal Newman, the 19th-century scholar/poet/musician/preacher/literary critic who is now on the road to sainthood, has become a symbol of the Catholic intellectual tradition. You might recognise his name from the Newman Centers on nearly every college campus in the US. His idea of the university reached back to the 'Studium generale', or school of universal learning, which he called 'the assemblage of strangers from all parts in one spot'.[4] There's an implied diversity and even expected discomfort that comes along with this use of the word 'strangers'. With all its potential for conflict, Newman's university of strangers was a place that 'created a pure and clear atmosphere of thought'.[5] Students weren't there passively to soak up knowledge, but to exercise 'the mind's energetic and simultaneous action upon and towards and among those new ideas, which are rushing in upon it'.[6]

Tempering the 'wild intellect'

From this Catholic perspective, the modern university should make room for diversity of thought. It should encourage these strangers to assemble so they may engage in that 'rationalistic exercise of reason'. But lately, there's been a movement to wash campuses of certain ideas and words that may be considered offensive, and it seems that rationality might get thrown out with them.

For instance, a professor can be fired for swearing in class. In 2015, Professor Teresa Buchanan was dismissed from her tenured position for saying 'fuck no' before her students, which Louisiana State University saw as part of a pattern of 'sexual harassment'.[7]

Even President Obama was not welcome to give a speech without an uproar. When Notre Dame invited Obama to give the school's commencement speech in 2009, several anti-abortion groups, students and alumni protested because they felt his pro-choice views were out of line with a Catholic university. The outrage gained a lot of traction. The local bishop, John D'Arcy, vowed to boycott the ceremony;

several alumni wrote letters of outrage; more than 70 Catholic bishops criticised the president of Notre Dame for inviting Obama; and more than 360,000 people signed a petition calling for the invitation to be rescinded.[8] In the end, Notre Dame never took back the invitation and Obama still addressed the graduates. It's a little ironic that someone would protest under the idea that pro-choice views are antithetical to Catholicism when, in fact, we know Catholic women have abortions at the same rate as other women.

Despite that, the anti-abortion side has devoted quite a bit of energy to silencing the voices and stalling the careers of people who could be creating that 'clear atmosphere of thought' around feminism and women's reproductive rights, especially on Catholic campuses. The Cardinal Newman Society – once called 'the most unhappily and inappropriately named society on the planet'[9] – is dedicated to raising a fit over so-called threats to universities' Catholicity. The Cardinal Newman Society devotes its energy to pointing out supposed breaches of dogma within Catholic universities; engineering negative publicity, primarily by instigating letter-writing campaigns; and posting online petitions. Anything from pro-choice professors and pro-LGBT events to *The Vagina Monologues* might be eliminated by negative publicity against school administrators.[10] Some administrations have refused to be cowed and have defended academic freedom, while others have listened to online furore or the local bishop and disinvited speakers and otherwise made their Catholic campus a smaller, more censorious place.

In July 2008, the University of San Diego (USD), a Jesuit Catholic institution, rescinded its offer of an endowed chair to Rosemary Radford Ruether, one of the most influential feminist theologians. The *National Catholic Reporter* once said that Ruether's 'scope is awesome' and a stack of her published books had to be measured next to a medium-sized person.[11]

Pamela Gray Payton, a USD spokesperson, claimed that Ruether's 'public position' on abortion was the primary reason for the rescinded offer. 'This chair is a powerful, visible symbol of Roman Catholic theology, and in Roman Catholic theology abortion is disallowed', she said.[12] Ruether thought there was an outside group that may have put pressure on the university. 'Its chief objection was my membership of the board of Catholics for Choice.'[13]

The fact that USD disinvited one of the most widely respected, published and read contemporary Catholic theologians was not lost on people in both the Catholic and academic worlds. Two Catholic organisations, the Women's Ordination Conference and Women's Alliance for Theology, Ethics and Ritual (WATER), organised a petition in protest and gathered over 2,000 signatures. 'Rosemary Ruether is like the godmother of the feminist theologian movement', said one of the endorsers.[14] Indeed, 56 faculty members at USD signed the petition.[15]

In this rescinded invitation, Ruether saw a worrying trend for the future of Catholic higher education: 'My concern is that Catholic colleges and universities are in danger of becoming intellectual ghettos where controversial issues, particularly in relation to Catholic teachings and practices, cannot be discussed. But if they cannot be discussed at Catholic universities, where else can they be discussed? What better place is there for them to be discussed?'[16]

I wonder, what was USD so scared of? It's the same old irony: excluding someone like Ruether is to acknowledge that her ideas are powerful.

Kowtowing to the censors

Though we know nothing of the shadowy complainers who initiated the USD controversy, they are not really the main problem. University administrators who cave in to an intimidation campaign are siding with censorship. Those who *answered* the call for restriction are the problem. After all, there is no controversy unless someone accepts it. If a university administration whittles their pedagogy down to little more than reading from a set of known truths, then universities are no longer a space for innovation, freedom or thought.

In 2012, Ohio state representative Bob Hagan was disinvited from speaking at the commencement for the Youngstown campus of the Mercy College School of Nursing. As an explanation, Bishop George Murry cited Hagan's pro-choice views. 'While I respect and appreciate many of the social-justice positions taken by Rep Hagan, it remains a fact that he also has consistently voted for pro-abortion legislation, policies and funding.'[17]

Hagan disagreed with the school's reasoning, pointing to his good works, which were in line with his Catholic faith. He remarked: 'I am saddened that the work that I have done to feed the poor, clothe the naked, help cure the sick, and to bring an end to the death penalty has fallen on deaf ears.'[18]

Murry offered to speak with Hagan, and they met for a 'cordial and respectful' discussion that touched on the role of individual conscience.[19] This meeting, however, was not enough to convince Murry to allow Hagan to speak or admit that he had made a mistake. Brian Corbin, diocesan director at the Office of Social Action at the Catholic Diocese of

Youngstown, all but admitted that they were scared of pro-choice ideas catching on: 'We are very concerned about issues of people who are actually public authorities that actually vote and they're elected.'[20]

Newman would have little patience for a Catholic university protecting a graduating class of nursing students from ideas. In fact, Newman would have wanted the bishop to debate side by side with Hagan. 'I want the same roof to contain both the intellectual and moral discipline', Newman wrote. 'Only a system that can tolerate and welcome such contradictions would be enough for students' "wild intellects".'[21]

Roxanne Martino, a business executive and Notre Dame alumna, resigned from the school's board of trustees in 2011, just two months after her appointment, when donations she made to pro-choice groups were made public. Conservative blogger Bill McGurn broke the story that she had donated more than $25,000 to Emily's List, a political action committee for pro-choice candidates. He also revealed Martino's donations to the Chicago Foundation for Women, which also supports pro-choice causes.[22]

In her official statement, Martino claimed she was resigning in 'the best interest of the university … I had looked forward to contributing in this new role, but the current controversy just doesn't allow me to be effective.'[23]

To add insult to injury, Notre Dame's trustees and president tried to manage the scandal by saying that Martino 'did not realise' that her donations were to pro-choice groups – as if depicting a savvy businesswoman as ignorant is somehow better than her support of reproductive rights.[24] McGurn criticised the Notre Dame administration for glossing over the very obvious pro-choice stance of Emily's List. 'It's sad that someone who obviously has enormous talents had to come to this kind of end. It's sadder still how the way [Notre Dame] handled it all put her in the worst possible light.'[25]

It's unclear how Martino's private activities – whether her giving history or any other personal decisions – should affect her ability to serve on the board of trustees of Notre Dame. Excluding a qualified alumna from a leadership position paints the Catholic university as a fragile thing. Surely a person making lawful decisions as a private citizen won't break the 'Studium generale', which is supposed to be welcoming – even to the opposition?

It may make for some noisy debates, but our society needs these multiple perspectives. This diversity means we are always free to change our minds – God forbid students never be allowed to change their mind about veganism or Marxism or even their major. As a result of engaging with opponents, we can become firmer in our convictions. The existence of committed adversaries forces both pro- and anti-abortion advocates to debate: to think deeply and speak clearly.

As the US Supreme Court has said, the university thrives on diversity of thought; it is the 'marketplace of ideas'.[26] It's disappointing when not everyone feels like that market should sell a wide variety of goods. As we have seen, groups like the Cardinal Newman Society use a straitjacket of uber-orthodoxy as a rallying cry against abortion and other reproductive rights, and the stories of Ruether, Hagan and Martino are becoming familiar. But as the censorious cleansing on campuses goes on, it isn't only pro-choice advocates who find themselves in the firing line – those opposed to abortion are also silenced. This should trouble all of us, no matter what our views on abortion or women's rights.

Censoring the anti-abortion side

In recent years, anti-abortion forces have devoted considerable energy to their protest tactics, which now include toting graphic displays of aborted fetuses on campuses around the country. These posters, or in the case of the Created Equal group, Jumbotron-sized displays, are designed specifically to goad the pro-choice side into a reaction.[27] For some pro-choice bystanders, this is taken as a visceral attack on their beliefs, and that's fine. Newman said that 'the energy of the human intellect does from opposition grow'.[28] However, it's hard to imagine him supporting those who try to block displays because they are upsetting or 'triggering' – and that is what some pro-choice advocates have done to anti-abortion campaigners on campus.

For example, an anti-abortion group was silenced at Johns Hopkins University (JHU) in 2015 over a display of fetal development. For the past 30 years, the JHU Voice for Life group had used the same display, which depicted the stages of fetal development, but suddenly the student committee determined that the display wasn't appropriate. 'We've reviewed your pictures with our advisers and have determined that your display contains triggering and disturbing images and content', said the student committee, banning Voices for Life from the university's spring fair. JHU Voice for Life president Andrew Guernsey responded, 'Abortion is disturbing, that's the reason we have such a table'. Guernsey pointed out that it was 'ironic that a university that has dedicated itself to the advancement of medicine and biology would find displaying medically accurate fetal models disturbing and offensive'.[29]

Ultimately, the student committee had second thoughts and reversed its ban. 'We were wrong in our initial decision', the committee said.

'The committee values free speech.'[30] The committee went on to clarify that JHU Voice for Life was not banned from the spring fair, only their fetal-development display.

In 2010, the Duke University Women's Center used similar reasoning when it cancelled an event planned by an anti-abortion group. Duke Students for Life (DSFL) planned to hold a 'Discussion with a Duke Mother' about the challenges of being a mother and student, as part of a 'Week for Life'. The day before the talk, DSFL received a voicemail notifying it that the discussion had been cancelled. Martin Liccardo of the Women's Center explained that the cancellation was because of a strong student backlash. 'We had a very strong reaction from students in general who use our space who said this was something that was upsetting and not okay. So based on that, we said, okay, we are going to respond to this and stop the programme.'[31]

The Foundation for Individual Rights in Education (FIRE), an independent watchdog group for free speech on campus, contested the university's decision. 'If Duke's promises of inclusiveness are honest, Duke must repudiate the Women's Center's decision and ensure that such viewpoint-based discrimination does not happen again', it wrote.[32] Within a day of FIRE's response, Ada Gregory, director of the Women's Center, issued an apology for the cancellation, although it was too late for the discussion to go forward. 'Mistakes were certainly made that should not have occurred', Gregory wrote to DSFL.[33] She continued, 'The Women's Center is intended to be a place that supports the agency and choices of all women'. In addition, Gregory invited Duke Students for Life to use the Women's Center facilities and join in events sponsored on campus.

FIRE executive director Robert Shibley summed up what happens when institutions give in to the contingent that has a hair trigger. In his view, the cancellation represented a 'deeply hypocritical violation' of the Women's Center's promise that it 'welcomes discordant viewpoints from varied experiences'.[34]

Censoring views you find objectionable can feel like the just thing to do. But one thing both the pro and anti sides can surely agree on is that it never feels just for the silenced minority. Silencing the opposition causes harm. Denying someone a voice can fuel a deep frustration, alienation and pain. An imposed silence has a way of turning into a shout and even a scream, because there is nothing more human than the need to be heard. The Catholic Church strives to cultivate a faith rooted in human dignity and equality, and there is no human dignity when we stop a woman or man from speaking about their lived experience.

In 2014, the Justice for All anti-abortion group displayed poster-sized images of aborted fetuses in the University of Georgia's Tate Plaza. The demonstrators were invited by the campus Students for Life group, according to member Fadi Greene: 'They have a tagline: "Abortion from debate to dialogue." And that's exactly what we want to do, have a dialogue with people.'[35]

There were several counter-demonstrations. The Women's Studies Student Organisation set up a table to offer condoms and literature on sexual health. However, several students took a more suppressive approach, by holding up bedsheets in front of the signs to block the images of fetuses from the view of passersby. Senior Stephanie Allerdice and junior Kimberly Brazis were among the students holding up a sheet. 'It's a graphic image people don't have to see ... it's a woman's choice, they don't have to be a victim to these tactics', said Allerdice. Brazis concurred: 'I think it's triggering and it's also shaming.'[36]

On British campuses, too, pro-choice campaigners have tried to silence anti-abortion student groups. In 2014, the Dundee University Students' Association (DUSA) refused to allow the Society for the Protection of Unborn Children (SPUC) to set up a stall at the university freshers' fair, even though SPUC had had a stall for the previous eight years[37]; the Oxford University Students' Union has stopped LIFE, an anti-abortion group, from advertising anywhere in the union[38]; and Cardiff University Students' Union discussed bringing in a pro-choice policy in 2015 that would effectively see all pro-life demonstrations banned from campus.[39]

In November 2014, a debate about abortion at Christ Church College, Oxford, was banned after 300 students threatened to turn up with 'instruments' to disrupt it: their complaint was that the debate featured two men, journalists Brendan O'Neill and Tim Stanley, the former due to make a pro-choice argument and the latter putting the pro-life case.[40] What's more, in 2012, University College London Union (UCLU) ruled that all discussions on abortion must include a pro-choice speaker, severely limiting the right of anti-abortion groups to associate with whom they please and to hold whatever kind of discussions they like.[41]

This is all deeply troubling. For Catholics, conscience takes a primary role. Conscience is our final arbiter – it's the reason I and many other Catholics believe that a woman can make a moral decision to end a pregnancy, to take birth control, to have *in vitro* fertilisation. If pro-choice people are committed to all women being able to follow their conscience, shouldn't we let the opposition follow theirs as well – even when it leads them to promote views we can't empathise with at all?

It seems logically impossible to support choice while preventing people from thinking for themselves, or while blocking opposing views with a bedsheet. Our position is strong enough that we don't need those kinds of narrow 'victories'. We should be able to debate the opposition and trust that students have the ability to judge for themselves which is the better argument. I think we will see that despite campaigns by the opposition, support for women's autonomy will always remain strong.

In fact, it doesn't help our argument to pretend that we're all marching in lockstep by silencing the other side, and it's simply not the truth. I would rather have anti-abortion supporters talk about their prejudices and feelings in front of me, so they can be examined in the light. An indicator that our ideas are strong and well-reasoned is our ability to deal with their arguments.

Some have argued that when we let the opposition question the bodily autonomy of women in a public space, we are giving into what some believe are the patriarchal foundations of society. But when you let the opposition voice an opinion that you don't agree with, it doesn't mean that idea becomes stronger. It doesn't mean that the idea becomes true. I would rather we talk openly through our differences and have a battle of ideas that questions how we see society.

Depicting debate as trauma

The fear that students in Catholic schools discussing different perspectives of the Catholic faith would somehow undermine religion is anathema to what it means to be Catholic. We are required vigorously to question and inquire with one another and live our religion. What's more, when pro-choice people on other campuses try to restrict debate on abortion, they undermine the very principle of moral autonomy which underpins our position. Wrapping students in cotton wool does a great disservice to their ability to engage with their beliefs.

I'm not saying people should not have visceral reactions to provocative protests. All positions on an issue deserve a continued and fervent rebuttal to make our students 'bolder, keener'. But the idea that we're all so traumatised by hearing an opinion that contradicts our lived experience or ideology infantilises us, and those whose rights we claim to protect.

When I look at the state of free speech in the academy, I am concerned that we are losing Newman's idea of the university as a curious place, one that houses that 'wild intellect'. It would be a shame for the university to go even further backward, to before the 12th century, and to look around and see that the 'Studium generale' had been lost and that strangers are no longer welcome.

Jon O'Brien *is the president of Catholics for Choice.*

Notes

1. 'The Religious Roots of Academic Freedom', by William J Hoye, *Theological Studies*, Vol 58, 1997, p. 415 cdn.theologicalstudies.net/58/58.3/58.3.1.pdf.
2. '"Ex corde" & the Medieval University', by Jean Porter, *Commonweal*, 7 June 2004, commonwealmagazine.org/misplaced-nostalgia-0.
3. 'Christianity and Scientific Investigation: A Lecture Written for the School of Science', by John Henry Newman, *Lectures and Essays on University Subjects*, 1858, newmanreader.org/works/idea/article8.html.
4. 'Discourse 4: What Is a University?', by John Henry Newman, In *The Idea of a University*, 1852, higher-ed.org/resources/newman-university.htm.
5. 'Discourse 5. Knowledge Its Own End', by John Henry Newman, In *The Idea of a University*, 1852, newmanreader.org/works/idea/discourse5.html.
6. 'Discourse 6: Knowledge Viewed in Relation to Learning', by John Henry Newman, In *The Idea of a University*, 1852, newmanreader.org/works/idea/discourse6.html.
7. 'LSU professor fired for using salty language in classroom claims she's "witch hunt" victim, plans suit', *Advocate*, 27 June 2015, theadvocate.com/news/12669113-123/lsu-professor-fired-for-using.
8. 'Obama Addresses Abortion Protests in Commencement Speech at Notre Dame', *Washington Post*, 18 May 2009, washingtonpost.com/wp-dyn/content/article/2009/05/17/AR2009051701622.html.
9. 'Catholic Identity: Real & Imagined', by Michael Sean Winters, *National Catholic Reporter*, 2 February 2011, ncronline.org/blogs/distinctly-catholic/catholic-identity-real-imagined.
10. 'The Cardinal Newman Society', Catholics for Choice, 2012, catholicsforchoice.org/news/pr/2012/documents/CardinalNewmanSocietywithlinks2012.pdf.
11. 'The life of "scholar activist" Rosemary Radford Ruether', by Mary E Hunt, *National Catholic Reporter*, 15 October 2014, ncronline.org/news/people/life-scholar-activist-rosemary-radford-ruether.
12. 'University of San Diego withdraws endowed chair appointment offer for pro-abortion professor', *Catholic News Agency*, 22 August 2008, catholicnewsagency.com/news/university_of_san_diego_withdraws_endowed_chair_appointment_offer_for_proabortion_professor/.
13. 'Intellectual Freedom and the Catholic University', by Rosemary Radford Ruether, *Conscience*, Vol XXIX, No 2, 2008.
14. 'USD revokes invitation to feminist theologian', *San Diego Union-Tribune*, 20 August 2008, utsandiego.com/uniontrib/20080820/news_lz1n20usd.html.
15. 'Amidst Protest, CNS Calls for Support of USD Admin Over Rescinding Offer to Pro-Abortion Theologian', *Catholic Education Daily*, 21 August 2008, cardinalnewmansociety.org/CatholicEducationDaily/DetailsPage/tabid/102/ArticleID/185/Amidst-Protest-CNS-Calls-for-Support-of-USD-Admin-Over-Rescinding-Offer-to-Pro-Abortion-Theologian.aspx.
16. 'Intellectual Freedom and the Catholic University', 2008.

17. 'Bishop George V Murry, SJ Statement On Mercy School Of Nursing Graduation', Catholic Diocese of Youngstown, 27 April 2012, doy.org/index.php?option=com_content&view=article&id=165.
18. 'Hagan Uninvited to Speak at Nursing School Graduation', WKBN News, 27 April 2012, web.archive.org/web/20120430154018/http://www.wkbn.com/content/news/local/story/Hagan-Uninvited-to-Speak-at-Nursing-School/bkAMe5HQuU2huz1K76qmgg.cspx.
19. 'Bp Murry and Rep Hagan Release Joint Communication', Catholic Diocese of Youngstown, 8 May 2012, doy.org/index.php/news-media/news-a-press-releases/168-bp-murry-and-rep-hagan-release-joint-communication.
20. 'Mercy College Disinvites Pro-Abortion, Pro-Gay Marriage Lawmaker at Ohio Bishop's Request', Catholic News Service, 1 May 2012, cnsnews.com/news/article/mercy-college-disinvites-pro-abortion-pro-gay-marriage-lawmaker-ohio-bishop-s-request.
21. 'Sermon 1: Intellect, the Instrument of Religious Training', and John Henry Newman, In *Sermons Preached on Various Occasions*, 1856, newmanreader.org/works/occasions/sermon1.html.
22. 'Roxanne Martino, Chicago Executive, Resigns From Notre Dame Board When Pro-Choice Support Exposed', by Joseph Erbentraut, *Huffington Post*, 9 June 2011, huffingtonpost.com/2011/06/09/chicago-executive-resigns_n_873828.html.
23. 'Chicago businesswoman resigns from Notre Dame board', *Chicago Tribune*, 8 June 2011, articles.chicagotribune.com/2011-06-08/news/ct-met-notre-dame-board-member-resign20110608_1_roxanne-martino-cardinal-newman-society-watchdog-group.
24. 'Handling of controversial trustee appointment raises questions about the university's mission', by Claire Gillen, *Irish Rover*, 30 August 2011, irishrover.net/?p=1155.
25. 'Roxanne Martino...', huffingtonpost.com/2011/06/09/chicago-executive-resigns_n_873828.html.
26. *Keyishian v Board of Regents*, 1967, law.cornell.edu/supremecourt/text/385/589.
27. 'Pro-life Group Uses Jumbotron to Broadcast Abortion Video on College Campuses', by Alexandra Desanctis, *College Fix*, 26 May 2015, thecollegefix.com/post/22599/.
28. 'Position of My Mind since 1845', by John Henry Newman, *Apologia pro Vita Sua*, 1865, newmanreader.org/works/apologia65/chapter5.html.
29. 'Johns Hopkins University reverses ban on pro-life display', *Christian Today*, 15 April 2015, christiantoday.com/article/johns.hopkins.university.reverses.ban.on.pro.life.display/52151.htm.
30. 'Johns Hopkins reverses ban on detailed pro-life display', by Maxim Lott, *Fox News*, 15 April 2015, foxnews.com/us/2015/04/15/johns-hopkins-reverses-ban-on-disturbing-pro-life-display/?cmpid=cmty_twitter_fn.
31. 'Duke Keeps Pro-Life Group Out of Women's Center During "Week for Life"', FIRE, 29 March 2010, thefire.org/duke-keeps-pro-life-group-out-of-womens-center-during-week-for-life-3/.
32. 'Duke Keeps Pro-Life Group...', thefire.org/duke-keeps-pro-life-group-out-of-womens-center-during-week-for-life-3/.
33. 'Duke University Women's Center Issues Apology to Pro-Life Group After Dustup', *Life News*, 30 March 2010, lifenews.com/2010/03/30/state-4938/.

34. 'Duke Keeps Pro-Life Group...', thefire.org/duke-keeps-pro-life-group-out-of-womens-center-during-week-for-life-3/.
35. 'Anti-abortion demonstration brings "constructive dialogue" to campus', *Red & the Black*, 3 March 2014, redandblack.com/uganews/campus/anti-abortion-demonstration-brings-constructive-dialogue-to-campus/article_52ad3fc8-a351-11e3-9be0-0017a43b2370.html.
36. 'Anti-abortion demonstration brings...', redandblack.com/uganews/campus/anti-abortion-demonstration-brings-constructive-dialogue-to-campus/article_52ad3fc8-a351-11e3-9be0-0017a43b2370.html.
37. 'Pro-life group banned from Scottish university's freshers' fair', *Catholic Herald*, 10 September 2014, catholicherald.co.uk/news/2014/09/10/pro-life-group-banned-from-scottish-university-freshers-fair/.
38. 'Pro-Life, Anti-Abortion Charity LIFE Banned From Advertising At Oxford University', *Huffington Post*, 4 June 2014, huffingtonpost.co.uk/2014/06/04/anti-abortion-charity-life-banned-advert-oxford-university_n_5443730.html.
39. 'The moral crusade against pro-life students', by Tom Slater, *spiked*, 26 November 2014, spiked-online.com/freespeechnow/fsn_article/the-moral-crusade-against-pro-life-students#.Vgrx_MtViko.
40. 'Abortion debate cancelled', *Oxford Student*, 20 November 2014, oxfordstudent.com/2014/11/20/abortion-debate-cancelled/.
41. 'Motion to the Emergency Members Meeting: Support a Student's Right to Choose – UCLU should be Pro-Choice', UCLU, uclu.org/sites/uclu.org/files/u2330/q2_proposal_version_jan_2012.pdf.

8

A Climate of Censorship:
Eco-Orthodoxy on Campus

Peter Wood

On 8 May 2015, the University of Western Australia (UWA) returned $4 million that the Australian government had designated for the creation of a 'consensus centre'. The university declined the funding because establishing the centre would have required the hiring of Danish environmentalist Bjorn Lomborg.

The university's decision stemmed from a campaign run in part by the UWA Student Guild. On 20 April, the Student Guild issued a manifesto titled, 'Bjorn Lomborg Has No Place at UWA'.[1] The guild's environment officer, Jessica Cockerill, explained that 'hundreds of UWA students, staff and alumni' were joining the protests, and that students were 'flocking' to a 'Say NO to Bjorn Lomborg' campaign.

Guild president Lizzy O'Shea had declared that, 'Students, staff and alumni alike are outraged'.[2] The centre of this outrage, according to O'Shea, was Lomborg's research, which 'downplays the effects of climate change and calls for inaction'.[3]

In O'Shea's view, the creation of a centre on campus linked to Lomborg would put the university's 'world-class reputation' at risk, and would be 'an insult to the staff and students', many of whom were already 'embarrassed to be associated with UWA' or 'ashamed that they have a degree from an institution that would accept someone like Dr Lomborg'.

O'Shea had reached out via Twitter and other media to a broader audience to whip up a campaign. 'Imagine paying $4 million to be lied to by a recognised fraud', one Twitter user, 'Lady Prudence', said. 'Just shows you that GO8 Universities will swim a sewer & kowtow to RWNJs Govt for$$$$#auspol', echoed another, named Christine Phillips.

Enough students were mobilised by the anti-Lomborg activists that the university's vice-chancellor folded. O'Shea exulted: 'It's a really good sign as far as community action goes that if enough people have mobilised against something, and don't support it, [then] people will change their minds.'[4]

Others drew different conclusions. Federal education minister Christopher Pyne called it 'a sad day for academic freedom'. Agriculture minister Barnaby Joyce observed that, 'Universities, they're supposed to be the crucible of allowing people to investigate and ponder an idea and come up with their own conclusions'.

The UWA's decision made news around the world and occasioned both celebration among climate activists and laments among supporters of intellectual freedom on campus. I'll come back to the expressions of both glee and woe. They speak powerfully about the new cultural dynamic that is evident in higher education throughout Western nations. But first, I would like to say a little about Lomborg, who was able to stir such passion long-distance, Australia being 8,843 miles from his home in Copenhagen. And I'd like to take note of the peculiar character of climate-change activism, which so eagerly embraces tactics of silencing and exclusion.

Lomborg's long afternoon

Lomborg is best known for his 2001 book, *The Skeptical Environmentalist*, in which he argued that many widely publicised predictions made by environmentalists were ill-founded. The book included a chapter which endorsed the idea that human activity contributes to global warming but disputed the then-popular forecast that the world would warm by six degrees centigrade by the end of the 21st century.

Lomborg, it appears, was right. Even the Intergovernmental Panel on Climate Change (IPCC), once a vigorous supporter of the forecast of a large increase in global temperature by the end of the 21st century, has changed its mind and drastically cut its predictions.

The Skeptical Environmentalist vaulted Lomborg to international celebrity and also made him the object of unrelenting attack by defenders of the predictions he disputed. He was singled out for his dissent on climate change. In 2003 the Danish Committees on Scientific Dishonesty (DCSD), under the authority of the Danish Ministry of Science, Technology and Innovation, took up three complaints from environmental scientists who considered Lomborg's views 'scientifically dishonest'. The DCSD ruled in January 2003 that Lomborg had misrepresented some scientific facts but was not dishonest. Lomborg appealed to the ministry, which annulled the finding of 'misrepresentation'. DCSD then dropped the matter.

These are the details that lie behind the anti-Lomborg talking points that he is a 'recognised fraud' or an 'embarrassment' to a university that upholds the search for truth.

In 2002, Lomborg founded the Copenhagen Consensus Center, a think tank that seeks 'solutions for the world's biggest problems by cost-benefit' analysis and 'data-driven prioritisation'. Generally it focuses on matters such as reducing world poverty and childhood mortality, though it includes 'climate change' among its 22 core research themes.[5] The centre's climate-change agenda focuses on persuading states to invest 0.5 per cent of their GDP in energy technology and another 0.5 per cent in helping 'hardest hit areas' to adapt. The centre argues against emission reduction targets on the grounds that they are not 'cost effective'.

These are positions that certainly do not mark out Lomborg as a purveyor of doubt about the theory of manmade global warming. Nor is Lomborg – a gay, vegetarian activist in what we Americans call progressive causes – by any stretch a social conservative, a champion of unfettered free markets or a proponent of other views that are generally in disfavour on the left. So why was he singled out for such vitriolic attack by the students at the University of Western Australia? If anything, Lomborg would appear to be an ally of the broader movement that has attacked him. In April 2015, just before the UWA Student Guild declared him *persona non grata*, Lomborg called for the elimination of all state subsidies for fossil fuels, on the grounds that cheap fossil fuels are 'exacerbating global warming'.[6]

But having once questioned the ruling orthodoxies on climate change, Lomborg became in the eyes of the movement's hard core something worse than a 'climate sceptic' or a 'denier'. He became a heretic. And in the years since he published *The Skeptical Environmentalist*, he has continued to attract fierce denunciation from those who can brook no dissent from the Established Church of Climate Catastrophe.

Jessica Cockerill, Lizzy O'Shea, and the other student activists at UWA who successfully kept Lomborg from being appointed to a position on the faculty, plainly did not concern themselves with the issues of academic and intellectual freedom. Lomborg's views were not welcome on campus, and indeed even the possibility of his kind of views being expressed amounted to an 'embarrassment'.

Beyond Lomborg

If this were an isolated incident, it might be written off as provincialism among students who were unacquainted with the principles of higher education and the ideals of free societies. That judgement wouldn't reflect well on the education their university had provided them, but it would keep the shadow of *L'affaire Lomborg* safely distant. But what happened at UWA is, unfortunately, more symptomatic than singular.

Lennart Bengtsson is one of the world's foremost climate scientists. He is a senior research fellow at the Environmental Systems Science Centre at the University of Reading and former director of the Max Planck Institute for Meteorology in Germany. He was part of the research team that won the 2005 René Descartes Prize for Collaborative Research for their work on climate and environmental change in the Arctic. Like Lomborg, Bengtsson has a long and deep history of concern for macro-environmental issues and, like Lomborg, Bengtsson could never be described fairly as someone who rejects 'climate change'.

But Bengtsson is also an independent thinker. As far back as 1990, he expressed his concern that the IPCC was exaggerating global warming. He noted that temperatures in the North Hemisphere had been, at that point, cooling for 40 years.[7] Then, in March 2014, Bengtsson co-authored a paper submitted to – and rejected by – *Environmental Research Letters*. The paper cast doubt on the IPCC's most recent projection of increases in global temperatures of 2 to 4.5 degrees centigrade by the end of this century. Moreover, it suggested that the world's climate might not be as sensitive to CO2 emissions as the IPCC's preferred models depict.

One of the reviewers responsible for the rejection of Bengtsson's paper privately wrote that he rejected it because its publication would hurt the climate consensus. It would be 'harmful' because 'it opens the door for oversimplified claims'.[8]

Bengtsson's troubles, however, were only beginning. He soon announced he was joining the advisory council of the Global Warming Policy Foundation, a UK body generally sceptical of the 'climate consensus'. He was immediately pilloried by the academic climate establishment and within days resigned from his post, writing that 'such an enormous group pressure in recent days from all over the world has become virtually unbearable to me'. He feared for his health and safety, he said:

> I see no limit and end to what will happen. It is a situation that reminds me about the time of McCarthy. I would never have expected anything similar in such an original, peaceful community as meteorology. Apparently it has been transformed in recent years.[9]

Because Bengtsson is an internationally renowned scientist, his case attracted widespread notice. But there are numerous other instances of dissenting scientists who have been subject to such persecution. My colleague Rachelle Peterson and I documented some of these – David Legates at the University of Delaware, James Engstrom at the University of California, Los Angeles – in our 2015 paper *Sustainability: Higher Education's New Fundamentalism.*[10]

But a stronger parallel is Wei-Hock 'Willie' Soon, a plasma physicist who has served as a non-tenured employee of the Harvard-Smithsonian Centre for Astrophysics since 1991, where he previously did his post-doctoral work. In 2003, Soon published a paper in *Climate Research* in which he argued that the twentieth century was not the warmest in the last millennium. The paper occasioned much controversy, and in 2011 Greenpeace, using documents obtained through Freedom of Information Act requests, attacked Soon for receiving over $1 million in funding from petroleum and coal interests.

In January 2014, Soon was the co-author of another paper, 'Why Models Run Hot: Results from an Irreducibly Simple Climate Model', which took exception to the 'consensus' climate models that predict significant global warming because of rising levels of carbon dioxide in Earth's atmosphere. In February, directly following the publication of this paper, the *Guardian* and the *New York Times*, making use of material provided by Greenpeace and 'an allied group', the Climate Investigations Centre, ran attacks on Soon for supposedly failing to disclose his sources of funding and for 'conflicts of interest'. This set in motion a widespread campaign to mark out Soon as a disgrace to the profession and someone whose scientific work should be ignored.[11]

Social justice vs. free speech

The ferocious attacks on climate sceptics represents the convergence of two trends: the new spirit of enforced conformity in the name of social justice, and the new fanaticism centred on a belief in an eco-apocalypse. I'll come back to censorship in the name of environmental correctness. To understand it, we need first to take the compass of the growing spirit of enforced conformity on a wider range of issues.

That spirit had been growing for several years on the feminist left when it was crystallised by Sandra Korn, an undergraduate women's studies major at Harvard. Korn, writing in the *Harvard Crimson* in February 2014, baldly declared that the 'liberal obsession' with academic free-dom was 'misplaced'. She wrote that academic freedom 'often seems to bump against something I think much more important: academic jus-tice'.[12] This was not just a statement of principle. Korn was ready with applications. Supporters of the idea that academic institutions should boycott Israeli universities should turn aside their opponents' concerns about academic freedom. They should insist that 'justice' is on the side of attacking Israel. Harvard's feminists should 'organise' to prevent government-studies professor Harvey Mansfield – a professor who held controversial views on gender roles and rape – from 'publishing further sexist commentary under the authority of a Harvard faculty position'. Academic freedom might permit him to praise 'ladylike modesty', but 'academic justice would not'. Korn also had praise for another effort to ensure the non-reappointment of an Indian instructor who had 'published hateful commentary about Muslims in India'.

Korn's declarations attracted wide notice – and criticism. The university still has a robust contingent that regards the freedom to seek the truth and to express one's views as a bedrock principle. But Korn's article nonetheless came as a revelation to many: there are students at elite universities who regard free speech as an unnecessary encumbrance. As Korn put it: 'If our university community opposes racism, sexism, and heterosexism, why should we put up with research that counters our goals simply in the name of "academic freedom"?'

The new climate

The Korn doctrine, if I can call it that, is just one manifestation of what Greg Lukianoff and Jonathan Haidt have dubbed a 'new climate' in higher education, a climate that 'is slowly being institutionalised'. Lukianoff and Haidt, in their 2015 *Atlantic* essay 'The Coddling of the American Mind', offer an explanation that emphasises that the 'current movement is largely about emotional wellbeing'. Students, raised in a time when parents had become overprotective and American life had become more politically polarised, are now 'more desirous of protection and more hostile toward ideological opponents than in generations past'. It is a world where 'acknowledging the other side's viewpoint has any merit is risky' because 'your teammates may see you as a traitor'.[13]

This psychological explanation of the 'new climate' has the merit of uniting several of the new forms of censoriousness. Lukianoff and Haidt observe the capacity of the social-media-savvy students to intimidate faculty by threatening 'their reputations and careers'; the elevation of emotional grievance over 'objective wrong'; the US Department of Education's Office for Civil Rights' needless expansion of the legal definition of sexual harassment to include 'verbal conduct that is simply "unwelcome"'; trigger warnings; training sessions to weed out 'microaggressions'; zero-tolerance policies; and disinvitations to speakers whom students judge to be offensive or likely to voice 'unsafe' ideas.

But, broad as it is, Lukianoff and Haidt's synthesis leaves a lot of things out. For one thing, the growing hostility to free speech in the university is not just an American thing. British universities are busy No Platforming dissenting views, even though British children have not had to endure 'helicopter parents' hovering overhead to protect them from life's little traumas.[14] Likewise, Jessica Cockerill and her anti-Lomborg activists at the University of Western Australia.

Existential anger

I have a somewhat different explanation for the generational change. The effort to silence opposing views by vitriolically denouncing them, and, if that fails, turning to physical assault, is the latest phase in the decades-long shift in Anglo-American societies from an ethic of emotional self-control to one of histrionic emotional display.[15]

The emotion that gets the greatest license in this shift is anger, which feels to the person expressing it 'empowering', righteous and authentic. That's a long story in its own right, but it has some immediate bearing.[16] If it is true, then Lukianoff and Haidt seem to have it backwards. The anger on campus directed at dissenters from favoured causes is not the result of students in the group hug feeling threatened; it is the *cause*. The students, bereft of both an emotional centre and a larger purpose, increasingly turn to ideologies that can provide a substitute for both: creeds of resentment. Rather than 'vindictive protectiveness' at work, what we see is pre-emptive belligerence. The angry person, boy or girl, needs something to be angry about. Many things can fit the bill: Black Lives Matter, the campus 'rape crisis', Palestinians, illegal immigrants ('DREAMers'), inequality, etc. The issues are disparate but their emotional dynamics are nearly identical. Each identifies a terrible injustice that has been not so much unnoticed as actively denied due attention by powerful, malevolent forces: structural racism, patriarchy, Islamophobia, Nativism, the One Per Cent. And, of course, Big Oil.

These malevolent forces use 'free speech' as a weapon but also disdain it as a disguise worn by their opponents. It is a weapon because they can manipulate supposed free speech to the disadvantage of the weak and oppressed, who are marginalised from any discussion of the issues that concern them. And it is a disguise because free speech tricks people into believing that the rich and powerful win by the merits of their arguments rather than by their hidden machinations.

This is why, per Sandra Korn's 'academic justice' doctrine, academic freedom is not to be trusted. If you have your values straight, you should ignore all those seductive appeals to listen to the best arguments on all sides and pay attention to the actual evidence. Argument and evidence are but the masks worn by the oppressors. Virtue lies in sticking with the cause, no matter what.

The fanaticism of the apocalypse

The Fanaticism of the Apocalypse: Save the Earth, Punish Human Beings is the English title of the French novelist and intellectual Pascal Bruckner's 2011 book on environmental catastrophism. Bruckner is a man of the left whose environmental views resemble Lomborg's. He holds that the doomsday scenarios favoured by the climate alarmists take attention away from problems that could be solved here and now, and injustices that need urgent attention.

Bruckner is a witty and sometimes aphoristic writer: 'Europeans have never been so concerned about the future as they have been since they stopped believing in it.'[17] He favours economic development: 'Several billion people expect growth and improvement in their lot. In the name of what could we dare deny it to them?'[18] And he sees the eco-apocalyptic view as a substitute creed for Westerners who have lost both Christianity and Marxism. In that light, 'Green puritanism may be nothing other than a reaction on the part of an irked West, the last avatar of a despondent neo-colonialism preaching to other cultures a wisdom it itself has never practiced'.[19]

Bruckner's accusation would astonish most American climate activists, who certainly don't see their movement as neo-colonialist in spirit or themselves as apologists for Western lifestyles. The environmental movement, in its own fine view, aims to save the planet. Some of the activists see this as a goal compatible with the continued use of fossil fuels and with economic development. These 'eco-modernists', however, are a minority. Climate-change activism as a whole proceeds in a spirit half in dread, and half in fond anticipation, of disasters that will bring the modern age of industrial development to a close.

This combination of dread and anticipation provides the rationale for shutting dissenters out of public discussion, on campus and off. Dissenters – those who express doubt about any part of the standard climate-change narrative – are now routinely labelled 'deniers' (or sometimes 'denialists') on the model of Holocaust deniers. The idea is that dissent from climate-change orthodoxy is not merely a mistake, but a moral outrage. Silencing them is therefore a moral duty.

Policing the 'consensus'

Often that sense of outrage is best glimpsed when someone manages to slip across the ideological picket lines and actually express a few words of scepticism. When the renowned physicist Freeman Dyson managed to slip into an interview on National Public Radio (NPR) the comment, 'I don't think the science is at all clear, and unfortunately a lot of the experts really believe they understand it, and maybe have the wrong answer', the climate-orthodoxy enforcers were indignant. Among the milder comments: 'Why are you giving this doddering dinosaur free advertising for his upcoming book? Why is NPR giving ANY airtime and credibility to a climate-change sceptic?'[20]

But for the distilled version of this view, we need to consider Naomi Oreskes and Erik Conway's little booklet, *The Collapse of Western Civilization: A View from the Future*. This is their imaginary view of world history from sometime in the 22nd century. Global warming has run amok due to carbon-dioxide emissions; the United States and other Western countries have collapsed after coasts flooded and hundreds of millions died. But it is not all bad. 'China's ability to weather disastrous climate change vindicated the necessity of centralised government' and inspired 'similar structures in other, reformulated nations'.[21]

Oreskes and Conway find this part of their fantasy especially delicious. 'Neocommunist China' weathers catastrophic global warming because it has authoritarian rule, while Western civilisation collapses due to 'neoliberals' who blocked 'anticipatory action'. In the West, 'individual freedoms' got in the way of fixing things; 'liberal democracy' proved an impediment; and a 'tiny elite who came to be known as the one per cent' eventually took charge. Thus in this vision of the future, the West destroys itself by putting too high a value on freedom.

Oreskes, professor of the history of science at Harvard, and Conway, the former historian of NASA's Jet Propulsion Laboratory at the California Institute of Technology, are better known for their previous book, *Merchants of Doubt: How a Handful of Scientists Obscured the Truth on Issues from Tobacco Smoke to Global Warming* (2010), and the documentary movie based on it. The book is an extended analogy between cigarette companies that in the 1950s raised doubts about the accuracy of studies that showed the health hazards of smoking and scientists today who express doubts about the most widely used models of manmade global warming. Analogy, of course, is not proof; it isn't even evidence. But it can be powerful rhetoric, and Oreskes is a widely credited source for the idea that critics of global-warming orthodoxy are merely shills for the fossil-fuel industry.

Delusional deniers

That's one way to rationalise the refusal to let the so-called deniers speak. Another comes from George Marshall, founder of the Climate Outreach and Information Network in Oxford. In *Don't Even Think About It: Why Our Brains Are Wired to Ignore Climate Change* (2014), Marshall finds that the deniers are only the most extreme expression of humanity's built-in tendency to ignore long-term threats and to huddle in groups that project their own version of reality. Climate sceptics are, in brief, delusional and outside the realm in which rational argument or evidence would matter. They practice 'social conformity' rather than independent thought.

Marshall's book is an elaborate screed against the very possibility of taking climate sceptics seriously. He locates the origins of such scepticism in the Tea Party, bullying extremists, and conservatives eager to 'replace the Red Menace bogeyman'.[22] Perhaps one of the oddest arguments he frames is that climate alarmists suffer from the problem that their movement 'lacks any readily identifiable external enemy', which makes it 'hard to motivate and mobilise people'.[23]

Marshall's entire book is about conjuring external enemies and rhetorically writing them off, and even as he proceeds with his alas-we-have-no-real-enemies conceit, he is simultaneously denouncing the 'disinformation campaign' of his opponents and attacking the 'nefarious' David and Charles Koch, the multi-billionaire brothers who are said to fund anti-environmental institutions and projects.[24]

There is a certain unintended hilarity in books such as Marshall's, in which a lack of self-awareness is paraded as sophisticated understanding. Marshall argues that lack of urgency about climate change is ultimately rooted in atavistic qualities we inherit from primitive ancestors. We are, he writes, 'so poorly evolved to deal with climate change'.[25] Perhaps condescension is one of the special adaptations of those who, like Marshall, have somehow evolved further.

Fresh air

Or, then again, perhaps he is mistaken. There is a substantial body of writing on the other side of the climate debate – the works of the so-called 'deniers' – that is more temperate in tone and more careful with the evidence. Virtually none of this makes it past the censors to be assigned in courses or discussed on campus, and the authors are never invited to speak. The barriers at this point are seemingly impregnable.

I'll nominate Ronald Bailey's recent book, *The End of Doom: Environmental Renewal in the 21st Century*, to stand for the dozen or so voices of climate scepticism published in just the last few years, not counting technical scientific works.[26] Bailey is a long-time observer of the failed predictions of the collapse of Western civilisation because of ecological disaster. He's not alone in this. Robert C Balling's *The Heated Debate: Greenhouse Predictions Versus Climate Reality* (1992) had questioned the 'global warming' thesis barely four years after its unofficial launch. It was 23 June 1988 when NASA scientist James Hansen testified in a hot Senate meeting room that, 'The greenhouse effect has been detected and it is changing our climate now'.[27]

The day was excessively hot and humid and the atmosphere in the meeting room was stifling. The situation was not, however, exactly what it seemed. The senator who arranged the hearing, Timothy Wirth, years later admitted that he called the Weather Bureau so that he could arrange the meeting on the hottest day of the year in Washington, and had his staff shut off the air-conditioning and open the windows to let the hot air in.[28]

Stagecraft, illusions and misrepresentation are, so to speak, in the genes of the climate-alarmist movement. Pre-empting open debate and fair consideration of contrary views was there from the beginning. The atmosphere in the Senate meeting room in June 1988 was sufficiently oppressive as to stifle free speech for more than a generation. Just ask Bjorn Lomborg.

Peter Wood *is the president of the National Association of Scholars.*

Notes

1. 'Bjorn Lomborg has no place at UWA', UWA Student Guild, 2014, uwastudentguild.com/bjorn-lomborg-has-no-place-at-uwa/.
2. 'WA students call for Bjorn Lomborg's $4m for climate research to be rejected', *Guardian*, 21 April 2015, theguardian.com/environment/2015/apr/21/wa-students-call-for-bjrn-lomborgs-4m-for-climate-research-to-be-rejected.
3. 'UWA vice-chancellor defends think tank linked to controversial environmentalist Bjorn Lomborg', ABC, 20 April 2015, abc.net.au/news/2015-04-20/vice-chancellor-defends-think-tank-centre-at-uwa/6407560.
4. 'Students praise UWA for ditching controversial $4m Bjorn Lomborg Consensus Centre think tank', ABC, 9 May 2015, abc.net.au/news/2015-05-09/students-praise-uwa-for-ditching-bjorn-lomborg-think-tank/6457210.

5. 'Research', Post-2015 Consensus, copenhagenconsensus.com/post-2015-consensus/research.
6. 'It's time to stop subsidizing fossil fuels', by Bjorn Lomborg, *Globe and Mail*, 17 April 2015, theglobeandmail.com/globe-debate/its-time-to-stop-subsidizing-fossil-fuels/article24002168/.
7. 'A Cool Blanket of Clouds', by Simon Rozendaal, *Elsevier*, 27 October 1990, In 'Bengtsson in 1990: "One Cannot Oversell the Greenhouse Effect"', *De staat van het klimaat*, 13 May 2014, staatvanhetklimaat.nl/2014/05/13/bengtsson-in-1990-one-cannot-oversell-the-greenhouse-effect/.
8. 'Scientists in cover-up of "damaging" climate view', by Ben Webster, *The Times*, 16 May 2014, thetimes.co.uk/tto/science/article4091344.ece.
9. 'Lennart Bengtsson resigns from the GWPF', by Judith Curry, *Climate Etc.*, 14 May 2014, judithcurry.com/2014/05/14/lennart-bengtsson-resigns-from-the-gwpf/.
10. *Sustainability: Higher Education's New Fundamentalism*, by Rachelle Peterson and Peter Wood, National Association of Scholars, March 2015, pp. 123–125, nas.org/projects/sustainability_report.
11. 'Two Controversial Professors', by Peter Wood, *Minding the Campus*, 14 June 2015, mindingthecampus.org/2015/06/two-controversial-professors/.
11. 'The Doctrine of Academic Freedom', by Sandra YL Korn, *Harvard Crimson*, 18 February 2014, thecrimson.com/column/the-red-line/article/2014/2/18/academic-freedom-justice/?page=single.
12. 'The Coddling of the American Mind', by Greg Lukianoff and Jonathan Haidt, *Atlantic*, September 2015, theatlantic.com/magazine/archive/2015/09/the-coddling-of-the-american-mind/399356/.
13. 'Have helicopter parents landed in the UK?', by Wendy Lee, *Guardian*, 9 October 2014, theguardian.com/education/2014/oct/09/have-helicopter-parents-landed-in-the-uk.
14. *A Bee in the Mouth: Anger in America Now*, by Peter Wood, Encounter Books, 2006.
15. 'Forgetting Freedom', by Peter Wood, *Claremont Review of Books*, Vol XV, No 3, 2015.
16. *The Fanaticism of the Apocalypse: Save the Earth, Punish Human Beings*, by Pascal Bruckner, Polity Press, 2013, p. 178.
17. *The Fanaticism of the Apocalypse*, p. 180.
18. *The Fanaticism of the Apocalypse*, p. 180.
19. 'A Veteran Scientist Dreams Boldly Of "Earth And Sky"', NPR, 2 May 2015, npr.org/2015/05/02/403530867/a-veteran-scientist-dreams-boldly-of-earth-and-sky.
20. *The Collapse of Western Civilization: A View from the Future*, by Naomi Oreskes and Erik M Conway, Columbia University Press, 2014, p. 52.
21. *Don't Even Think About It: Why Our Brains Are Wired to Ignore Climate Change*, by George Marshall, Bloomsbury, 2014, p. 38.
22. *Don't Even Think About It*, p. 39.
23. *Don't Even Think About It*, p. 41.
24. *Don't Even Think About It*, p. 46.
25. *The End of Doom: Environmental Renewal in the 21st Century*, by Ronald Bailey, Thomas Dunne Books, 2015.

26. 'Years Later, Climatologist Renews His Call for Action', by Andrew Revkin, *New York Times*, 23 June 2008, nytimes.com/2008/06/23/science/earth/23climate.html?_r=0.
27. 'Interviews: Timothy Wirth', Frontline Politics, PBS, 24 April 2007, pbs.org/wgbh/pages/frontline/hotpolitics/interviews/wirth.html.

9

Terrorism and Free Speech: An Unholy Alliance of State and Students

Tom Slater

> For too long, we have been a passively tolerant society, saying to our citizens: as long as you obey the law, we will leave you alone. This government will conclusively turn the page on this failed approach.[1]

So said Conservative prime minister David Cameron, in a speech made just after he was returned to power at the 2015 UK General Election. Having spent the past five years in coalition with the Liberal Democrats, during which Tory reforms on counterterrorism and surveillance had been stalled by inter-party politicking, the gloves, it seemed, were coming off.

Alongside beefed-up powers to store communications, revoke passports and rescind citizenship, Cameron unveiled plans to stem the influence of extremism on university campuses. Under Section 26 of the Counter-Terrorism and Security Act – which received Royal Assent in February 2015 – universities would be required to give 'due regard to the need to prevent people from being drawn into terrorism'.[2] In practice, this means a programme of censorship and surveillance, with universities charged with being the moral guardians of, and informers on, their own staff and students.

In another speech, in September 2015, made just before the new conditions were to come into place, Cameron made assurances his plans would not amount to censorship. 'It is not about oppressing free speech or stifling academic freedom', he said. 'It is about making sure that radical views and ideas are not given the oxygen they need to flourish.'[3] But anyone with a liberal bone in their body could see through the doublespeak: the government was mandating what students would be able to hear, read, say and think. State censorship was once again casting a shadow over British academia, only a few months after Cameron had marched with other world leaders on the streets of Paris in solidarity with the slain *Charlie Hebdo* cartoonists.

This was a long time in the coming. For decades, the Home Office has banned terrorist groups outright and made espousing support for them, on campus or anywhere else, a criminal offence. But the government's controversial Prevent Strategy has had a particularly insidious impact on university campuses. Established by New Labour in 2003, as part of the counterterror CONTEST programme, Prevent set out to strike up partnerships with public institutions and community groups in order to stem the influence of terrorism, facilitate surveillance of 'at-risk' individuals, and refer potentially dangerous individuals to the government's de-radicalisation programme, Channel.[4]

The first few years of Prevent were deeply controversial. Not only was it criticised by civil libertarians; right-wingers were also up in arms, claiming Prevent had allocated funds to extremist organisations.[5] When the Conservative-led coalition came to power in 2010, it pledged to reform Prevent and take a much tougher stance. When it was relaunched in 2011, the remit of Prevent had been extended, shifting the focus from terrorism to 'extremist (and non-violent) ideas that are also part of a terrorist ideology'. Public institutions – including schools, prisons and universities – were urged to be far more vigilant in rooting out and referring potential extremists.[6]

The revamped Prevent Strategy was bad news for free speech on campus. The given definition of non-violent extremism – 'vocal or active opposition to fundamental British values, including democracy, the rule of law, individual liberty and mutual respect and tolerance of different faiths and beliefs' – was worryingly broad.[7] In theory, expressing traditional religious beliefs or radical political ideas could put a target on your back, and, inevitably, Muslim students would bear the brunt of the scrutiny.

For the first few years, universities' obligations under Prevent were vague and unenforced, but this all changed with the arrival of the Counter-Terrorism and Security Act. Establishing a so-called Prevent Duty in law, it put universities' counterterror responsibilities on a firm, statutory footing. Universities were now required to tighten up external-speaker policies, monitor their students, filter internet access, give counter-extremism training to staff and liaise with local Prevent coordinators and the police.[8]

The Prevent Duty prompted a huge backlash from universities, academic unions and student campaigners. The University and College Union (UCU) passed a motion at its 2015 congress stating that the

Prevent Duty 'seriously threatens academic freedom and freedom of speech' and 'legitimise[s] Islamophobia and xenophobia'.[9] While students' unions, as private charities, are not subject to Prevent's provisions, the National Union of Students (NUS) resolved to lobby against the new Act, arguing that the government's plans would erode civil liberties and result in the 'further alienation and disaffection' of Muslim students.[10]

This response was welcome. But it wasn't all it seemed. As *spiked*'s 2015 Free Speech University Rankings revealed, 80 per cent of universities and students' unions censor speech. These bodies were decrying state censorship while carrying out their own censorship on an industrial scale. The only difference was the targets they chose. While the government took aim at so-called non-violent extremists, universities and SUs frequently No Platformed inflammatory politicians, 'transphobic' feminists and un-PC comedians.[11]

You could call this a question of priorities: petty, individual bans might look trifling next to systematic state censorship. But this ignores the role UK universities and students' unions have played in setting the stage for the state to step in. Freedom of speech is an indivisible liberty, and by making their own concessions, universities and students' unions have made it near impossible for them to argue against Prevent on the basis of principle. But the problem runs deeper than mere double standards. Over the past few decades, campus politicos and university bureaucrats have imbued censorship with moral legitimacy. This is the high ground that the government is now trying to claim for itself.

As this chapter will explore, the phoney war over Prevent obscures the much deeper crisis we face. Homegrown terrorism is a significant problem in the UK. Over the past few years over 700 British citizens have fled to the Islamic State.[12] And among them were university graduates like Mohammed Emwazi, who after leaving the University of Westminster in 2010 found international notoriety as the masked executioner Jihadi John.[13] More than ever, Islamist ideas need to be debated and demolished, and the case for liberalism and democracy needs to be remade. Universities should be among the main arenas in which this battle of ideas is had out. But, as we will see, both the government and universities themselves have made it almost impossible for this to happen.

Lessons in censorship

In the frenzied response to the Prevent Duty, one unassuming statement, issued by Universities UK chief executive Nicola Dandridge, stuck out. 'All universities', she said, 'have procedures and protocols that have to be satisfied before external speakers are given the green light to speak at a campus event'.[14] Dandridge's nonchalance was jarring, but appropriate. For all their screeching, universities and students' unions have, for decades, presided over byzantine bureaucracies designed to regulate everything from external speakers to 'appropriate IT use'. And, within these policies, the bar for censorship is often incredibly low. Forget 'non-violent extremism': the University of Bristol's external-speaker policy forbids 'needlessly offensive or provocative action and language'.[15]

All of this pre-dates Prevent. Unlike the US, where public universities are bound to uphold free speech as a matter of law, UK universities are, effectively, required to curtail it. Section 43 of the Education (No2) Act (1986) imposes a duty on universities to 'take such steps as are reasonably practicable to ensure that freedom of speech within the law is secured for members, students and employees of the establishment and for visiting speakers'.[16] But given that, from hate-speech legislation to equality duties, UK law curtails free speech in myriad ways, risk-averse universities routinely over-interpret their legal obligation to restrict speech. In the end, Prevent merely adds another layer to an already-laden legal framework.

Universities and student campaigners have not only done nothing to challenge the illiberal status quo – they've also been more than willing to censor speakers on their own terms. Indeed, universities have even, on occasion, censored Islamists – just for different reasons to the government. In November 2014, the University of East London banned Islamic preacher Imran Ibn Mansur, stating that his openly homophobic views 'go against our equality policies'.[17] In February 2015, the LGBTI Society at the University of Westminster led a campaign to have Islamic cleric Haitham al-Haddad banned over comments he made about homosexuality and the 'right' way to carry out FGM.[18] In the end, the talk was suspended by the university following a media storm over the revelations that Jihadi John had studied at Westminster.

Similarly, students' union censorship has been explicitly used by the government to communicate and justify its own censorious measures. The NUS's longstanding No Platform policy, which bans members of racist and fascist organisations from speaking on campus,[19] is praised in the 2011 Prevent Strategy as a 'largely effective' means of challenging extremism.[20] And the new *Counter-Extremism Strategy*, published in October 2015, more or less cribs the language and logic of No Platform entirely: 'We must be careful to only give a platform to the right people.

We will be absolutely clear about the people and groups we will not deal with because we find their views and behaviour to be so inconsistent with our own.'[21] That No Platform should prove such a big influence on the government should come as no surprise – indeed, the NUS has always been ahead of the curve in spotting, and banning, dodgy political groups. In 1994, Islamist group Hizb ut-Tahrir – which even the government is yet to ban – was added to the No Platform list.[22]

In these and many more instances, the logic of government intervention is mirrored in existing campus programmes. As I explore elsewhere in this volume, students' unions have, over the last few years, begun policing crude forms of sexual expression – from clumsy come-ons to lewd pop songs – in the name of stamping out sexual assault. The idea is that hypersexualised, laddish expression constitutes a 'rape culture' that affirms 'rape-supportive attitudes' and can lead men to commit heinous acts.[23] This deeply insidious idea is akin to the 'slippery slope' rhetoric of Prevent. As David Cameron put it in a speech in July 2015: 'You don't have to support violence to subscribe to certain intolerant ideas which create a climate in which extremists can flourish … No one becomes a terrorist from a standing start.'[24] This is the same alarmist sentiment with different prejudices attached.

The portrayal of students as passive imbibers of ideas and influences has fuelled and affirmed the project of Prevent. If students are thought of as so easily influenced, censorship comes to be seen as a moral necessity. And the government's de-radicalisation programme, Channel, springs from the same paternalistic logic. Where, in the past, radicals were seen as people who made a conscious decision to take up a particular cause or set of beliefs, they are presented in government literature as brainwashed victims – 'vulnerable persons' who are corrupted by a 'radicalising influencer'.[25] This passive conception of the individual is now thoroughly mainstream in academic and students' union circles.

Even the UCU and NUS ripostes to the government's plans revealed just how much they had common with Cameron's censorious regime. While both organisations paid lip service to the principles of free speech and academic freedom, they seemed more concerned that the plans would send 'the wrong message' to the population at large. UCU claimed that Prevent 'legitimises Islamophobia and xenophobia, encouraging racist views to be publicised and normalised within society',[26] while the NUS wrung its hands over how Prevent 'reinforces stereotypes that have had a strongly negative impact on some of our most vulnerable community members'.[27] Once again, individuals are presented as irrational, easily led and volatile. Even in this supposed free-speech fightback, the logic of censorship pervades.

Since the arrival of the Counter-Terrorism and Security Act, it's become common for student activists to hold Prevent up as the *real* threat to free speech on campus. As one student op-ed put it: 'If free-speech activists would like to superficially address the merits and limits of political correctness, go ahead – but the real threat to freedom of expression is still at large.'[28] Yet, while state censorship must always be of primary concern, we cannot ignore the role universities and students' unions have played in providing a justification for government intervention. Universities and students' unions have not only legitimised campus censorship – they have contributed to the culture of vulnerability on which the Prevent Strategy is built. Unless campus groups wake up to their own hypocrisy and argue from a position of principle, then it will be near impossible for them truly to challenge Prevent.

The perversion of tolerance

When David Cameron announced the introduction of the Prevent Duty in September 2015, he marked the occasion by naming and shaming universities that had hosted extremist speakers. King's College London, the School of Oriental and African Studies (SOAS) and Queen Mary were among the institutions that were said to have collectively hosted over 70 such events in the previous year.[29] It was a cheap PR stunt, but it rammed something home: extremism clearly is a problem on campus. In the heart of our most respected universities – institutions founded on liberal, Enlightenment values – students are being attracted to some of the most backward ideas imaginable. And the fact that a proportion of them have since taken the journey to Syria proves we cannot be complacent.

Cameron has said that 'all public institutions have a role to play in rooting out and challenging extremism',[30] and, in part, he's right. Universities should be places in which no idea is allowed to fester unchallenged and where groupthink – whether it's among feminists or Islamists – is punctured through candid and confident discussion. However, what Cameron is incapable of grasping is that more debate, not less, is the solution. We need to uproot, debate and demolish the ideas underpinning Islamist extremism. We need to treat extremism as a set of ideas that should be debated, not a virus to be contained. We *do* need to challenge extremism – but censorship is no challenge at all.

The government may well recognise that Prevent is doomed to fail. The history of censorship teaches us that pushing bad ideas underground does nothing to stem their influence – if anything, it emboldens the sense of grievance that bigots and extremists have always traded in. As one academic remarked, Prevent is, at best, a short-term containment activity.[31] Nevertheless, the government's willingness to clamp down on freedom in the name of protecting it does speak to a tremendous confusion about the meaning and purpose of liberal, democratic values. This is what needs to be confronted before any concerted effort to challenge Islamism can be made.

In this regard, tolerance is perhaps the most misunderstood value of all. 'We must be intolerant of intolerance' is a common refrain in political discourse today. Indeed, it is reflected in one of Cameron's favourite counterterror catchphrases: that we have become 'passively tolerant' of extremism.[32] This represents a profound perversion of the meaning of real tolerance. In his *Letter Concerning Toleration* (published in 1689), John Locke made a strident case for tolerating religious faiths at a time of intense tension and persecution. But this was not borne out of passivity, of a desire to live and let live. Many of the religious views Locke felt should be tolerated he also considered batty and ungodly. What he recognised was that reason and judgement, rather than coercion and censorship, were the answer. 'In teaching, instructing, and redressing the erroneous by reason', he wrote, we can 'do what becomes any good man to do'.[33]

Today, tolerance has become decoupled from challenge and debate. It has, as Frank Furedi has argued, 'been redefined as a polite gesture of non-judgementalism'[34] – and this confusion permeates both sides of the Prevent debate. While the government refuses to tolerate extremism, campus officials work to ringfence it from criticism. Universities often – as Cameron's PR stunt shows – turn a blind eye to Islamist speakers. But, at the same time, they routinely censor those who criticise Islamism. For instance, secularist campaigner Maryam Namazie was banned from giving a talk at the University of Warwick Students' Union in September 2015 (a national outcry later caused it to reconsider), because it claimed her views were 'inflammatory' and could 'incite hatred' against Muslims.[35]

The paradox here is that, as a self-avowed feminist and human-rights campaigner, Namazie probably has more in common with the SU officials who banned her than the Islamists whose feelings they were trying to protect. Here, non-judgemental tolerance collides with a paternalistic obsession with protecting 'marginalised' groups from offence. It's a confounding, relativistic worldview that often expresses its 'liberal' credentials by stopping others from advocating liberal views.

Propounding our values becomes a secondary concern to ensuring that minority groups do not feel that their own values are coming under undue attack. One writer, reflecting on the Namazie ban, summed up the sentiment well: 'In looking out for British Muslims, the left is [not] abandoning its traditional values. In fact it's doing what it's always tried to do – extending a hand to the most beleaguered among us, identifying those society says it's okay to injure and insult, and saying: this isn't fair.'[36]

While this might sound terribly noble, it is profoundly patronising. From this perspective, Muslims are presented as uniquely volatile and thin-skinned, suggesting they are physically incapable of allowing their views to be challenged. What's more, as Namazie has pointed out, the desire to censor those who oppose Islamism – a specific political ideology – for the sake of protecting *all* Muslims represents a pretty offensive conflation. 'They've bought into this idea that a Muslim equals an Islamist, and that there's no difference between Islam, the religion, Islamism, a part of the religious right, and Muslims, who are people with as different a range of beliefs as anybody else', she said.[37]

This perversion of tolerance has allowed Islamist extremism to fester and grow. State censorship has worked to push it underground, emboldening its message and keeping it away from challenge. But the response from student and academic leaders has been just as damaging. By dampening down debate on these issues in the name of tolerance and equality, they have lent Islamists their own echo chamber.

British values

A central plank of the government's counterterror strategy is the promotion of so-called British values. While this has struck a sour, jingoistic note for many, what the given definition boils down to is an inoffensive approximation of liberal-democratic values, namely 'democracy, the rule of law, individual liberty and mutual respect and tolerance of different faiths and beliefs'. Now, a government espousing what it deems to be shared values is no bad thing. But that's not what's going on here. The government is not 'promoting British values' – it is trying to enforce them. And, by trying to protect freedom and tolerance by denying it to certain sections of the population, the government shows just how compromised these values are.

The academy is affected by a similar loss of faith. The modern university is established on the principles of free inquiry and the pursuit of truth. But not only are universities today all-too-willing to undermine these principles, they have become incapable of defending the liberal tradition itself. Of course, universities should be spaces in which all ideas should be interrogated. But even liberal academics seem incapable of sticking up for liberal-democratic values. In an article for the *Washington Post*, postgraduate student Avinash Tharoor discussed arriving to study at the University of Westminster in 2010, a year after Mohammed Emwazi had graduated. Extremism was rife on campus, and yet academics were terrified of challenging it. In one shocking anecdote, a niqab-clad student rejects Kant's democratic theory in a seminar on the grounds that 'as a Muslim, I don't believe in democracy'. It was not so much this admission but what followed that most shocked Tharoor: 'Our instructor seemed astonished, but did not question the basis of her argument; he simply moved on.'[38]

This retreat from Enlightenment ideas – in the face of the rise of Islamist extremism – is a double tragedy. Not only is free speech being curtailed, denying us of the opportunity to challenge extremist ideas in open debate. But this profound unravelling of Western values, at the heart of institutions that are supposed to defend them, will only enhance the appeal of Islamist ideas. As Bill Durodié has argued, homegrown terrorism emerges from a 'domestic cultural confusion' in which 'we are all engaged in a search for purpose and meaning due to the failure of contemporary society to provide any coherent direction'.[39] As Western society has become hollowed out, individuals are sent looking for purpose and direction. Tragically, some have found it in the deadest of dogmas. That Islamism is flimsy, bigoted and opportunistic – exploiting grievance and identity, rather than offering an inspiring, positive vision – shows just how fragile Enlightenment values have become.

The phoney war over Prevent is not only awash with double standards – it also obscures the crisis of Western society itself. At precisely the time when the values of the Enlightenment face a profound, international challenge, a time when debate has to be thrown open about the future direction of society, we find speech reined in and academics unable to articulate the purpose of their own intellectual tradition. For all the well-founded fears about state censorship, Prevent will make little difference to the state of free speech on campus. So-called British values have already withered from within.

Tom Slater *is deputy editor at* spiked *and coordinator of the Free Speech University Rankings.*

Notes

1. 'Cameron to set out new laws to tackle radicalism', Reuters, 13 May 2015, uk.reuters.com/article/2015/05/13/uk-britain-militants-idUKKBN0NX 2OW20150513.
2. Counter-Terrorism and Security Act 2015, Legislation.gov.uk, legislation.gov. uk/ukpga/2015/6/contents/enacted/data.htm.
3. 'UK universities face legal duty to halt student radicalisation', *Financial Times*, 17 September 2015, ft.com/cms/s/0/f7ac900c-5c8f-11e5-a28b-50226830d644.html#axzz3pxtn0oH4.
4. *CONTEST: The United Kingdom's Strategy for Countering Terrorism*, HM Government, July 2011, gov.uk/government/uploads/system/uploads/attachment_data/file/97994/contest-summary.pdf.
5. *When Progressives Treat with Reactionaries: The British State's flirtation with radical Islamism*, by Martin Bright, Policy Exchange, 2006, policyexchange.org.uk/images/publications/when%20progressives%20treat%20with%20reactionaries%20-%20jul%2006.pdf.
6. *Prevent Strategy*, HM Government, June 2011, p. 6, gov.uk/government/uploads/system/uploads/attachment_data/file/97976/prevent-strategy-review.pdf.
7. *Prevent Strategy*, p. 107, gov.uk/government/uploads/system/uploads/attachment_data/file/97976/prevent-strategy-review.pdf.
8. *Prevent Duty Guidance: for higher education institutions in England and Wales*, 2015, HM Government, gov.uk/government/uploads/system/uploads/attachment_data/file/445916/Prevent_Duty_Guidance_For_Higher_Education__England__Wales_.pdf.
9. *The Prevent duty: a guide for branches and members*, University and College Union, July 2015, p. 4, ucu.org.uk/media/pdf/8/i/Prevent_duty_guidance_Jul15.pdf.
10. 'Statement on Counter-Terrorism and Security Bill', NUS Connect, 14 January 2015, nusconnect.org.uk/articles/statement-on-counter-terrorism-and-security-bill.
11. Free Speech University Rankings, 2015, spiked-online.com/fsur.
12. 'Who are Britain's jihadists?', BBC News, 18 September 2015, bbc.co.uk/news/uk-32026985.
13. 'Islamic State: Profile of Mohammed Emwazi aka "Jihadi John"', by Dominic Cascianai, BBC News, 8 March 2015, bbc.co.uk/news/uk-31641569.
14. 'Students should back anti-radicalisation strategy, says David Cameron', *Daily Mail*, 17 September 2015, dailymail.co.uk/wires/pa/article-3238000/Students-anti-radicalisation-strategy-says-David-Cameron.html.
15. 'Freedom of Speech Policy 2015/16', University of Bristol, bristol.ac.uk/media-library/sites/secretary/documents/student-rules-and-regs/freedom-speech-policy.pdf.
16. Education (No2) Act 1986, HM Government, legislation.gov.uk/ukpga/1986/61/section/43.
17. 'London university bans preacher who calls homosexuality a "filthy" disease', *Evening Standard*, 24 November 2014, standard.co.uk/news/london/london-university-bans-preacher-who-calls-homosexuality-a-filthy-disease-9879579.html.

18. 'Westminster University students try to stop "homophobic" cleric speaking', *Guardian*, 23 February 2015, theguardian.com/education/2015/feb/23/university-westminster-students-homophobic-preacher.
19. 'No Platform policy', National Union of Students, 2014, s3-eu-west-1.amazonaws.com/nusdigital/document/documents/15029/a0f269f0c17f1c ccfdeffd840ef2e336/NEC_140916_Paper%203.3_No%20platform%20policy v2.pdf?AWSAccessKeyId=AKIAJKEA56ZWKFU6MHNQ&Expires=144614249 1&Signature=1g%2Babw%2F41fkKRtUGufdCHu7N0kU%3D.
20. *Prevent Strategy*, p. 74, gov.uk/government/uploads/system/uploads/attach ment_data/file/97976/prevent-strategy-review.pdf.
21. *Counter-Extremism Strategy*, HM Government, October 2015, p. 32, gov.uk/government/uploads/system/uploads/attachment_data/file/470088/51859_Cm9148_Accessible.pdf.
22. 'No more "good" or "bad" Muslims', by Jennie Bristow, *Times Higher Education*, 2 August 1996, timeshighereducation.com/news/no-more-good-or-bad-muslims/99681.article.
23. 'NUS finds "startling" lack of sexual harassment policies on campuses', *Guardian*, 27 July 2015, theguardian.com/education/2015/jul/27/nus-finds-startling-lack-of-sexual-harassment-policies-on-campuses.
24. 'Extremism: PM speech', Gov.uk, 2015, gov.uk/government/speeches/extremism-pm-speech.
25. *Counter-Extremism Strategy*, HM Government, October 2015, p. 21, gov.uk/government/uploads/system/uploads/attachment_data/file/470088/51859_Cm9148_Accessible.pdf.
26. *The Prevent duty: a guide for branches and members*, p. 4 ucu.org.uk/media/pdf/8/i/Prevent_duty_guidance_Jul15.pdf.
27. 'Statement on Counter-Terrorism and Security Bill', nusconnect.org.uk/articles/statement-on-counter-terrorism-and-security-bill.
28. '"Prevent" is the real free speech issue', by Husna Rizvi, *Varsity*, 9 October 2015, varsity.co.uk/comment/8971.
29. 'British universities that give the floor to extremist speakers are named and shamed', *Telegraph*, 17 September 2015, telegraph.co.uk/education/universityeducation/11870429/British-universities-that-give-the-floor-to-extremist-speakers-are-named-and-shamed.html.
30. 'British universities that give the floor to extremist speakers are named and shamed', telegraph.co.uk/education/universityeducation/11870429/British-universities-that-give-the-floor-to-extremist-speakers-are-named-and-shamed.html.
31. 'Securitising Education or Losing Direction?', by Bill Durodié, In *British Journal of Educational Studies*, 2016.
32. 'David Cameron to unveil new limits on extremists' activities in Queen's speech', *Guardian*, 13 May 2015, theguardian.com/uk-news/2015/may/13/counter-terrorism-bill-extremism-disruption-orders-david-cameron.
33. *A Letter Concerning Toleration*, by John Locke, 1689, constitution.org/jl/tolerati.htm.
34. 'No, Cameron, you can never have "too much" tolerance', by Frank Furedi, *spiked*, 19 May 2015, spiked-online.com/newsite/article/no-cameron-you-can-never-have-too-much-tolerance/16987#.VjJCf7fhC70.

35. 'Student union blocks speech by "inflammatory" anti-sharia activist', *Guardian*, 26 September 2015, theguardian.com/education/2015/sep/26/student-union-blocks-speech-activist-maryam-namazie-warwick.

36. 'There's nothing misguided about the left's concern for Muslims', by David Shariatmadari, *Guardian*, 1 October 2015, theguardian.com/commentisfree/2015/oct/01/university-of-warwick-maryam-namazie-activist.

37. 'If Islamists can speak on campus, why can't I?', by Tom Slater, *spiked*, 29 September 2015, spiked-online.com/newsite/article/if-islamists-can-speak-on-campus-why-cant-i/17486#.VjJDQ7fhC70.

38. '"Jihadi John", a graduate of my radical university', by Avinash Tharoor, *Washington Post*, 27 February 2015, washingtonpost.com/opinions/jihadi-john-a-graduate-of-my-radical-university/2015/02/27/2e36ea64-bde4-11e4-8668-4e7ba8439ca6_story.html.

39. 'Prevent: a very risky strategy', by Bill Durodié, *spiked*, 19 March 2015, spiked-online.com/newsite/article/prevent-a-very-risky-strategy/16793#.VjJENLfhC70.

10
Academic Freedom: The Threat from Within

Frank Furedi

Universities have always faced pressure to fall into line with the world-view of dominant political forces. Until the 1980s, the main victims of attacks on academic freedom were university teachers who expressed controversial views and who fell foul of influential political and economic interests. Back then, the main threat to academic freedom was from sources that were external to university life. In the contemporary era, however, the assault on academic freedom is increasingly being waged from within the institutions of higher education. In recent decades, there have been direct attacks on academic freedom from within universities themselves. It is no longer merely illiberal political voices that call for the silencing of dissident academics or the banning of controversial speakers; now, university administrators, teachers and students are often in the forefront of policing speech on campuses

Within higher education, there is a disturbing mood of intolerance towards those who hold unconventional or unpopular opinions, particularly in relation to politics. Some academics and their students do not simply challenge views that they dislike or find intolerable; they often seek to ban them and prevent the individuals who advocate them from working or speaking on their campuses. An issue like the troubled relations between Israel and Palestine is no longer a subject of open discussion and debate on campus. Instead, both sides in this controversy seek to deny their opponents the right to free speech and ban speakers with whom they disagree.

The shift from an external threat to academic freedom towards an internal undermining of that liberty has important implications for the whole culture of higher education. What it indicates is that academic freedom has lost its status as a fundamental principle governing university life. For many in the academic community today, academic freedom is not really a cause worth fighting for. At best, it is regarded pragmatically as a second-order value, which can often be trumped by more important considerations. At worst, academic freedom is treated as a negative value – as an outdated principle that upholds the privilege of powerful elites and which therefore has to be curbed in order to protect more powerless members of society.

The indirect challenge to academic freedom

In modern times, most societies have recognised that their futures depend on the development of science and knowledge, and that these things can only be developed through the free pursuit of ideas by scholars and scientists. Academic freedom endows all members of a university with the right to express their views freely. It allows them to teach views that they deem fit, and to research and publish their findings. This freedom is widely acknowledged as being essential to the pursuit of knowledge. As a 1998 report by UNESCO observed: 'Since the accumulation of knowledge through enquiry is a condition of human progress and advance, academic freedom is a condition of that progress.'[1]

Intellectual and scientific progress requires a culture that is disposed to open debate and to the spirit of experimentation. Academic scholars and scientists must have the freedom to follow their research in whatever direction it takes them. Moreover, academic freedom is not simply a means to an end. Since it provides the conditions for intellectual development and flourishing, it is a positive value in its own right. Regardless of its outcome, the freedom to think, talk, teach and research fosters a climate that encourages the realisation of the human potential.

Historic breakthroughs in intellectual and scientific thought inevitably challenge the prevailing order. And those who question convention frequently face repression and gain the attentions of the censor. Since the 19th century, the ideal of university autonomy and the liberty of those involved in higher learning to teach, research and express their views have been formally upheld in many societies. In some cases – for example, Austria, Estonia, Finland, Germany, Spain, Sweden – academic freedom is affirmed in a nation's actual constitution. Although it is a privilege that is frequently confined to the institution of the university, such freedom to inquire and discuss should not be seen as an eccentric, outdated or corporate right. Everyone benefits from the exercise of this freedom. It encourages the development of science and knowledge, which benefits the whole of society.

As an abstract ideal, academic freedom continues to enjoy significant cultural validation. UNESCO has gone so far as to declare that academic freedom is 'not simply a fundamental value' but also 'a means by which higher education [fulfils] its mission'.[2] Given the prestige enjoyed by the ideal of academic freedom, attempts to undermine it or limit its scope are rarely expressed in an explicit and open manner. Indeed, even those who propose the policing of freedom of speech on university campuses will declare their unswerving support for academic freedom. As one American commentator has noted:

> Because academic freedom is an extremely powerful and popular notion, few, if any, public universities promulgate detailed prospective speech regulations. Indeed, many universities spell out academic freedom guarantees in faculty contracts or in binding rules published in university handbooks. However, the very same universities who 'guarantee' the academic freedom of their employees also promote guidelines and codes of conduct that regulate the speech, writing and research of academics.[3]

University guidelines on speech and codes of conduct do not directly question the authority of academic freedom. As David Bernstein points out, 'The threat of censorship remains, however, when universities adopt extremely vague guidelines banning "harassment" based on race, sex, and other attributes'.[4] This indirect regulation of behaviour and speech means that a formal adherence to the principle of academic freedom can coexist with conventions and rules that implicitly contradict it.

One reason why academia rarely perceives codes of conduct, the subjugation of research to the pronouncement of ethics committees, and various rules affecting speech and expression, as threats to traditional academic freedom is because these attacks are rarely formulated in an explicit, self-conscious form. Qualifications on the exercise of academic freedom are invariably communicated through the narrative of hints and asides. Time and again, the rhetorical affirmation of academic freedom is coupled with qualifications which insist that this freedom is not absolute. Such claims often express social, moral and ethical concerns that apparently justify limiting academic freedom.

The juridification of university life is the most important medium through which the indirect policing of academic freedom takes place. Since the 1980s there has been a proliferation of rules, codes of conduct and guidelines that regulate every aspect of university life. Often such guidelines are used as quasi-legal instruments to limit and regulate academic investigation. The demand that academics adhere to such rules is often made in technical language, in order to bypass the more substantive issue of values and principles. In the US, and increasingly in the UK, academics are told to fall in line with these rules in order to avoid lawsuits.

Since rules and procedures often seem like neutral management instruments, their corrosive impact on academic freedom is rarely noted. Yet the constant expansion of process in the academy, of informal and formal rules, has nurtured a climate in which academic freedom is continually compromised by the spread of bureaucratic micromanagement. The standardisation of evaluation procedures, benchmarking, auditing, quality-assurance procedures – all of these compel academics to act according to a particular script. The institutionalisation of such practices doesn't only undermine the exercise of professional discretion and judgement – it also compromises the ability of academics freely to pursue their teaching. Sadly, academics rarely challenge the introduction of processes and regulations that compromise the free pursuit of knowledge and research.

Insofar as academic freedom is debated today, it is rarely talked about in relation to these indirect attacks on its integrity. It is only when there is an explicit demand to censor an art exhibition or to ban a speaker that media commentators or politicians raise concerns about the standing of academic freedom. This focus on the occasional external challenge to academic freedom coexists with a relative degree of indifference to the more pervasive, routine and institutionally sanctioned curbs on the right of academics to express and conduct themselves in accordance with their ideas and scholarship.

Subordinating academic freedom to other values

Since the 1970s, universities have become increasingly prescriptive and have imposed an ever-expanding range of values on their members. An examination of the mission and core-values statements of universities throughout the Anglo-American world shows that these documents leave little to chance. Consider the 'Core Values Framework' of Birmingham City University. The values are excellence, a focus on people, partnership, fairness and integrity.[5] The university website asserts that these core values 'define the qualities most important to us and provide guidance for all that we do in order to enrich our teaching and learning environment'.[6] However, one conspicuous absence in this 'Core Values Framework' is academic freedom.

Some universities include a watered-down version of academic freedom in their values statements. For example, the University of Cambridge lists 'freedom of thought and expression' alongside 'freedom from discrimination' as some of its core values.[7] However, the proliferation of values through the constant enactment of codes of conduct diminishes the real status of academic freedom. Academic freedom has become one value among many, and is often seen as being on a par with the convention of being polite and respectful to others. Moreover, the rules of conduct devalue and even negate the principle of academic freedom in two important ways. The regulation of conduct, teaching and research activities implicitly limits the capacity of academics to exercise their formal freedoms. More importantly, the codification of certain regulatory values can and often does contradict the exercise of academic freedom.

One of the most dramatic ways in which the status of academic freedom has been devalued is through the sanctification of the value of not offending members of the university. The convention that words and ideas that some people find offensive must be regulated is now widely endorsed and institutionalised throughout higher education. Virtually every university in the UK has adopted rules of conduct or codes of practice that convey the message: 'The student must not be offended.' The policing of the speech of academics and students is underwritten by specific codes of conduct on language. Such codes invariably insist that staff and students should always be sensitive to the feelings of others.

The exhortation to 'watch your words' is not merely a piece of helpful advice. For example, Liverpool Hope University warns that it 'expects those in staff management or student-support roles to help staff and students carry out the terms of this policy'.[8] Line managers policing staff to ensure that they are sensitive to each other's feelings is unlikely to create a climate favourable to the flourishing of the free exchange of ideas. The university's policy statement warns that it 'may take appropriate steps under its harassment policy when language is used to harass or bully'. Since perceptions of linguistic harassment are inherently subjective, virtually any serious clash of views can become a punishable offence.

Liverpool Hope University's policy statement assumes that the value of 'inclusive language' overrides that of free speech. Consequently, this institution has assumed moral authority for guiding the verbal communication and exchanges of its members. The document states: 'Liverpool Hope recognises that language is not static and aims to ensure that staff and students are aware of changes and developments in language-use as they relate to equal opportunities, particularly in the area of language and offence.'[9]

The sanctification of the value of inclusive, non-offensive language serves as a justification for restraining the speech of academics. No doubt institutions like Liverpool Hope formally endorse the value of academic freedom. But the deification of the commandment Do Not Offend has transformed academic freedom into a freedom of not offending. There is little doubt that academic freedom can make life uncomfortable for teachers and students alike. Often the pursuit of the truth leads in unexpected directions and calls into question cherished beliefs and conventional wisdom. And, of course, words and the ideas they express can offend. Yet serious intellectual debate often involves criticising and questioning people's cherished beliefs. Radical and novel ideas can challenge the worldview of individuals to the point where they feel that their way of life, culture or identity is being attacked and undermined. In such circumstances, the views of academics may well be perceived as personal attacks or interpreted as disrespectful and offensive. But without the right to offend, academic freedom becomes emptied of its positive experimental and truth-seeking content.

The devaluation of academic freedom is demonstrated in the fact that higher education has devoted far more energy to curbing its scope than it has to affirming its value. Despite its rhetorical affirmation, academic freedom is rarely embraced as a non-negotiable value that underpins the genuine pursuit of intellectual and scientific clarity. Increasingly, the refrain 'academic freedom is not absolute' communicates the message that it can be subordinated to other, apparently more important, ideals and causes.[10] It seems that while academic freedom has become contingent on whether or not its exercise provokes a bad reaction, the right not to be offended has acquired the status of an absolute principle.

There are powerful cultural forces at work that promote the perception that the policing of academic freedom is not what it really is: the coercive regulation of everyday communication and the repression and stigmatisation of certain ideas. Instead, the undermining of academic freedom is often presented as an enlightened attempt to prevent offence or as a sensible way of minimising conflict.

Sadly, some academics have been at the forefront of advocating curbs on freedom of expression on the grounds that words are weapons that can traumatise and psychologically damage people. Some have gone so far as to argue that the risks posed by free speech are far greater in higher education than in other domains of life.

Mari Matsuda, a professor of law, has claimed that universities are a 'special case' where there must be protection from hateful and offensive speech. Why? Because, according to Matsuda, 'the typical university student is emotionally vulnerable'.[11] She added that 'students are particularly dependent on the university for community, for intellectual development and self-definition'. Consequently, 'official tolerance of racist speech in this setting is more harmful than generalised tolerance in the community at large'.[12] The claim that university students require special protection from offensive speech is perverse. Precisely the site that needs to have a robust approach to free speech is the one where its exercise is now deemed to be uniquely threatening to the self-esteem of students.

In effect, the right of academics to freedom of expression competes with the right of students not to be offended. From this perspective, the regulation of academic life is not seen as a form of authoritarian intrusion but as a sensible measure designed to protect the vulnerable from pain. The idea that language offends is not new. But the notion that because offensive speech can have a damaging impact on people it must be closely regulated represents an important departure from the way it was viewed in earlier times. We're witnessing a radical redefinition of human subjectivity. The new undermining of free speech and academic freedom assumes that people – particularly students, and especially those from minority communities – lack the psychological and intellectual resources to deal with competing ideas. In such circumstances, controversial ideas are redefined as psychologically harmful, and their suppression is represented as an act of public service.

The aspiration to protect individuals and people from painful words is underwritten by a powerful cultural outlook. Consequently, today there is only a feeble affirmation for academic freedom in practice, however much it might still be formally nodded to. Indeed, one often gets the impression that academics and public figures are more interested in criticising the ideal of free speech than they are in upholding it.

Academic freedom becomes a second-order value

Despite the formal adherence of institutions of higher education to the ideal of academic freedom, this principle has in practice become a second-order value. Its begrudged acceptance as something useful to the development of science and scholarship coexists with ambivalence towards its idealisation as a foundational principle. In effect, academic freedom has become a negotiable commodity that is subordinate to other concerns.

The instrumental use of academic freedom is even embraced by individuals who are contemptuous of it as a real value. One academic blogger, Robin Marie, who believes that the ideology of social justice outweighs the principle of academic freedom, describes academic freedom as a 'liberal shibboleth'. Nevertheless, Marie recognises that appeals to this liberal shibboleth can be useful. She notes that the 'cultural clout of appealing to freedom of speech and evoking the ideal of the fearlessly critical space of higher education provides powerful tools to those hoping to advance dissenting views'. However, this 'cultural clout' is only useful insofar as it promotes the author's cause – which in her case is that of social justice.[13] Marie has little enthusiasm for academic freedom as such, and in her instrumental appeal to this principle she exudes contempt for the liberal shibboleth of free speech.

Critics of the 'liberal shibboleth' of academic freedom are careful not to go so far as to call for its abolition. The reason for their qualified critique is that, while they are happy to deny academic freedom to their opponents, they fervently uphold their own right to free thought and speech. The case of the American academic Steven Salaita is instructive in this respect. Salaita has been in the forefront of the campaign to prevent Israeli scholars from participating in academic conferences and research projects in the US. He is in no doubt that the principle of academic freedom does not extend to his political opponents. However, when the University of Illinois decided to withdraw the offer it made to employ him as a professor in the American Indian Studies programme, Salaita and his supporters were outraged that his academic freedom had been violated. In this instance at least, the 'liberal shibboleth' of academic freedom was transformed into a sacred principle.

The title of an article published in the *Harvard Crimson* in February 2014 succinctly expressed today's subordination of academic freedom to other principles. It read: 'Let's give up on academic freedom in favour of justice'.[14] What is significant about this contribution is that it not only treated academic freedom as a second-order principle; it also depicted it as an obstacle to the realisation of apparently more important values. According to the author of this article, silencing the voices of those academics whose ideas offend students is a small price to pay for upholding what she characterises as 'academic justice'.

Characteristically, aversion towards genuine tolerance and academic freedom on campuses is expressed through the narrative of double standards. From this perspective, academic freedom is an entirely negotiable commodity. Instead of perceiving it as a fundamental principle governing academic life and scholarly research, this freedom is reduced to a second-order value, which may give way to more lofty concerns. As the author of the *Crimson* article said, 'When an academic community observes research promoting or justifying oppression, it should ensure that this research does not continue'.

Until recent times, critics of academic freedom tended to argue that although they regarded it as a very fine principle, they felt that there were clear limits to its application. In the current era, critics of academic freedom are openly scathing about the values that it embodies. The language with which the *Crimson* article framed the concept of academic freedom was full of contempt and disdain. Throughout the piece, academic freedom was constantly coupled with the term 'obsession'. The assertion that those who take academic freedom seriously are misguided fools was justified on the grounds that academic freedom has no real content. According to the author, this 'liberal obsession' is in any case 'misplaced', since 'no one ever has "full freedom" in research and publication'. The conviction that academic freedom is an unhealthy obsession is by no means a view limited to the undergraduate who wrote that article.

Explicit rejection of academic freedom

Most of the time, critics of academic freedom tend to question it indirectly. Often individuals who attack the academic freedom of their foes still claim the rights it encompasses for themselves. For example, proponents of academic justice do not call for the abolition of academic freedom, merely its subordination to their own values. Nevertheless, there is a discernible tendency towards the rejection of the very essence of academic freedom.

The most coherent opponents of the ideal of academic freedom are often illiberal academics who are wedded to the belief that this principle simply reinforces the marginalisation of the powerless. They claim that academic freedom is monopolised by those who possess privilege and the power to flourish at the expense of those who require special protection. From this standpoint, what is required is not freedom but the regulation of academic activity.

In America, anti-discrimination codes are used to protect people from the 'hostile environment' on campuses supposedly created by the offensive behaviour and speech of 'privileged' individuals. Barbara White, a University of New Hampshire women's studies professor, denounced academic freedom in the following terms:

> Academia ... has traditionally been dominated by white heterosexual men and the First Amendment and Academic Freedom (I'll call them

FAF) have traditionally protected the rights of white heterosexual men. Most of us are silenced by existing social conditions before we get the power to speak out in any way where FAF might protect us. So forgive us if we don't get all teary-eyed about FAF. Perhaps to you it's sacrosanct as the flag or the national anthem; to us, strict construction of the First Amendment is just another yoke around our necks.[15]

In recent times, the view that academic freedom is a privilege enjoyed by a powerful group of university elites has gained in influence.

One of the most regrettable consequences of the tendency to present academic freedom in a negative light is that it has actually enhanced a sense of insecurity and powerlessness among students. The representation of free speech and offensive ideas as threats to people's wellbeing, and as potential sources of trauma, has gained influence over campus culture. In effect, the demand for trigger warnings and Safe Spaces can be interpreted as a call to be protected from the perils posed by the exercise of academic freedom.[16]

Unlike students in the past, undergraduates today are far more likely to campaign for the regulation of academic freedom than for its expansion. The infantilising message that 'the student must not be offended' has been internalised and in many cases codified in numerous institutions of higher education. Indeed, the culture of insulating students from offensive or disturbing ideas has become so pervasive that it has been unthinkingly embraced by sections of the undergraduate community. The infantilisation of undergraduates has succeeded to the point where sometimes it is the students themselves who demand to be protected from disturbing thoughts. On many campuses, it is student advocates and not insecure campus administrators who are at the forefront of promoting calls for trigger warnings on class syllabi. What's fascinating about the advocacy of trigger warnings in universities is that it represents the first time that young students are demanding the moral policing of their own reading material. Unsurprisingly, many academics are concerned that their own students are demanding the introduction of practices that they regard as a threat to academic freedom.

Yet unless ideas and arguments have a capacity to challenge prevailing conventions and disturb their audience they are unlikely to amount to very much. The pursuit of scholarship and the clash of views it promotes will inevitably upset some members of the academic community. But the flourishing of higher education needs individual risk-takers who are ahead of their time and prepared to search for the truth, wherever it may lead and whomever it may offend. A serious higher-education institution does not seek to limit academic freedom; it affirms it, in principle and in practice. It should regard academic freedom as a non-negotiable value that underpins the genuine pursuit of intellectual and scientific clarity. It should teach its members how not to take uncomfortable views personally and not to be offended by them.

Frank Furedi *is a sociologist and author of books including* Power of Reading, On Tolerance *and* Where Have all the Intellectuals Gone?.

Notes

1. *Autonomy, Social Responsibility and Academic Freedom*, UNESCO, 1998, p. 13, unesdoc.unesco.org/images/0011/001173/117320e.pdf.
2. *Autonomy, Social Responsibility and Academic Freedom*, p. 9, unesdoc.unesco.org/images/0011/001173/117320e.pdf.
3. *You Can't Say That!: The Growing Threat To Civil Liberties From Antidiscrimination Laws*, by David E Bernstein, Cato Institute, 2004, p. 67.
4. *You Can't Say That!*, p. 67.
5. 'Our Core Values Framework', Birmingham City University, bcu.ac.uk/cmsproxyimage?path=/_media/docs/core_values_framework.pdf.
6. 'Jobs with us', Birmingham City University, bcu.ac.uk/about-us/job-hunters/core-values.
7. 'The University's mission and core values', University of Cambridge, cam.ac.uk/about-the-university/how-the-university-and-colleges-work/the-universitys-mission-and-core-values.
8. 'Equal Opportunities Policy – Statement of Inclusive Language Use', Liverpool Hope University, hope.ac.uk/media/liverpoolhope/contentassets/documents/personnelforms/policiesandforms/media,1063,en.pdf.
9. 'Equal Opportunities Policy', hope.ac.uk/media/liverpoolhope/contentassets/documents/personnelforms/policiesandforms/media,1063,en.pdf.
10. See: 'Academic Freedom of Professors and Institutions', by Donna R Euben, American Association of University Professors, 2002, aaup.org/issues/academic-freedom/professors-and-institutions.
11. 'Public Response to Racist Speech: Considering the Victim's Story', by Mari Matsuda, In *Words That Wound: Critical Race Theory, Assaultive Speech, And The First Amendment*, Mari Matsuda et al (eds), Westview Press, 1993, p. 44.
12. 'Public Response to Racist Speech', p. 44.
13. 'Thinking Critically About Academic Freedom: The Case of Salaita', by Robin Marie, Society for US Intellectual History, 4 June 2015, s-usih.org/2015/06/thinking-critically-about-academic-freedom-the-case-of-salaita.html.
14. 'The Doctrine of Academic Freedom', by Sandra YL Korn, *Harvard Crimson*, 18 February 2014, thecrimson.com/column/the-red-line/article/2014/2/18/academic-freedom-justice/.
15. Quoted in: 'Second Thoughts on Sexual Harassment', by Paul Trout, Montana Professor, mtprof.msun.edu/Spr1994/TrArt.html.
16. 'On Trigger Warnings', American Assoication of University Professors, August 2014, aaup.org/report/trigger-warnings%20.

Conclusion: How to Make Your University an Unsafe Space

Tom Slater

The explosion of Safe Spaces on university campuses shows where censorship leads if you let it run rampant. That is, nowhere. Political, intellectual and scientific progress relies on the free exchange of ideas, on allowing the space for bad, old ideas to be challenged and good, new ideas to emerge. Safe Spaces are not only censorious – they're cowardly. They encourage students to barricade themselves in with the likeminded, wallow in their own self-righteousness, and never bother with trying to engage with, let alone change, the world around them.

Safe Spaces originated in women's and gay liberation groups in the 70s and 80s. Even then they were not without their problems, but they were, at the very least, outward-looking. They offered a place in which individuals could take a step back, formulate their ideas and then go back out into the world and change things for the better. They were a means, rather than an end. Now, the Safe Space *is* the end. The greatest achievement is retreat.

If students and academics want to change the world, rather than seal themselves off from it, then they need to turn their universities into Unsafe Spaces – places where any idea, no matter how offensive, challenging or disturbing, can be aired and contested. Here's how to do it.

Say no to No Platform

Banning a speaker you disagree with is a cop-out. Telling someone to shut up doesn't change their mind. And sticking your fingers in your ears and saying 'la, la, la, you're not there' doesn't mean you've won the argument. All this does is push dodgy ideas out of sight and save you the bother of having to articulate and stand up for your own. If you disagree with someone, argue with them, and trust in the audience to make up their own minds.

Reject the right to be comfortable

Once, radicals demanded the right to vote, the right to abortion on demand and the right, above all, to express themselves. That the demand of today is the right to be comfortable – from the 'emotional harm' of bad ideas – tells you about everything you need to know about modern student politics. If you want to be emotionally comfortable, go back to bed, or the womb. The real world can be a pretty uncomfortable place. If you want to live in it, you'd better get used to it.

Shoot down trigger warnings

As a method of helping PTSD sufferers recover from trauma, trigger warnings are misguided. As a mandatory learning tool, they're utterly disastrous. There are plenty of ideas that trigger strong responses – that's usually an indication that there's something to them. If you want to understand the world around you, you've got to embrace being 'triggered'. And if you take yourself seriously as a thinker, you should not insist on being treated like a child. Trigger warnings are the Parental Advisory stickers of academia. Reject them.

Keep the state out of free debate

If the history of free speech teaches us anything, it's to not trust the state with protecting it. In these times of panic and uncertainty, it is all too easy for the government to chip away at our liberties. Challenge it, fight back – always. But you've got to practice what you preach. You can't ban hate preachers and then complain when the government bans a different set of hate preachers. You need to argue from a position of principle.

Have a laugh

It's not enough to dismiss campus censors as killjoys and fun sponges. But sometimes they just are. The war on banter, the banning of un-PC Halloween costumes and the regulation of 'inappropriately directed laughter' are all cases in point. The most puritanical and ludicrous refrain of the modern campus politico, so often uttered before they ruin someone else's harmless fun, is 'banter is *not* just banter'. Well, actually it is. That's why we call it banter. Never stop making fun of them.

Education not re-education

You come to university to debate and to learn, not to be told how to behave. The campus rape panic has created a toxic climate in which dictating to young people how they should think about sex and what they should do in the bedroom has become completely acceptable. Young men are not all sex-criminals-in-waiting, and young women don't need to be protected from their clumsy come-ons. Stick up for yourselves, and call time on consent classes.

Down with academic justice

When activists say that academic freedom is a sham, that it props up bigotry and inequality, and that we should throw it out in favour of academic justice – ignore them. They still want academic freedom – they just want it for themselves only. Our entire intellectual tradition is built on the idea that, if you want your ideas to win the day, you have to make your case and make it well. Academic justice is the slogan of the sore loser and the lazy thinker.

The debate is *never* over

There are no four words more chilling to intellectual debate than these: the debate is over. As celebrated as an idea may be, as much as we might cherish a particular social gain, we should never ringfence it from criticism. When we do, we turn our beliefs into prejudices, inherited ideas that we believe to be true without really knowing why. But you can never be sure. History is full of people getting things wrong. Let your opponent speak – maybe you'll learn something.

Index

abortion, 22–3, 61, 81–90
academic freedom, 53–6, 75–7, 81–2, 118–28, 131
academic justice, 55, 77, 97–100, 125–6, 131
Achebe, Chinua, 65
Adorno, Theodor, 48–9
Alberti, Leon Battista, 18
al-Haddad, Haitham, 109
American Association of University Professors, 64, 70, 71, 77
American Studies Association, 70

Bailey, Ronald, 103
Balling, Robert C, 103
Barghouti, Omar, 70–1, 74, 75, 78
Bengtsson, Lennart, 96
Bernstein, David, 120
Bindel, Julie, 28–9
Birmingham City University, 121
Bloomberg, Michael, 75, 76
'Blurred Lines', 11, 24
Boycott, Divestment and Sanctions, 68–79, 98, 125
Brandeis University, 6
Brendan O'Neill, 22, 31, 78, 88
Brooklyn College, 75–6
Brown University, 12
Bruckner, Pascal, 100

Cameron, David, 106–7, 110, 111–12
Campus Sexual Assault Study, 39–40
capitalism, 48–51
Cardiff University, 6, 25, 37, 88
Cardinal Newman Society, 83, 86
Catholicism, 81–2, 88–9
Chait, Jonathan, 8, 11, 12
Columbia University, 6, 23, 28, 73, 74
consent, 23, 26, 41–2, 43, 131
Conservative Party, 10, 11–12
Conway, Erik, 101
counter-terrorism, 106–14, 130

Counter-Terrorism and Security Act, 106–7, 111
critical theory, 48–51

Dapper Laughs, 25, 37
Dartmouth University, 12
democracy, 8–9, 30–1, 107–8, 112–13
Derrida, Jacques, 50
Duke University, 87
Durodié, Bill, 114
Dworkin, Andrea, 29, 52
Dyson, Freeman, 101

Education (No2) Act, 109
Eminem, 10
Emory University, 12, 13
Emwazi, Mohammed, 108, 109, 114
Enlightenment, 8, 16–18, 51, 113–14
environmentalism, 93–103
Erdely, Sabrina Rubin, 36, 39

feminism, 11, 22–31, 51–3
Firefly, 62
First Amendment, 14, 30, 37, 53, 126–7
Foucault, Michel, 49–50
Foundation for Individual Rights in Education, 2, 25, 64, 87
Frankfurt School, 48–9
fraternities, 34–43
Free Speech Movement, 1, 42
Furedi, Frank, 112

Game of Thrones, 62
Gould, Jon, 11–14
Great Gatsby, The, 8, 28, 58, 65
Greenpeace, 97
Greer, Germaine, 3, 6

Hagan, Bob, 84–5
Haidt, Jonathan, 98, 99
harmful speech, 2, 5–7, 12, 15, 29, 47–8